◆ *Pot Luck* ◆

◆ *Pot Luck* ◆

A Celebrity Cookbook

PELHAM BOOKS

First Published in Great Britain by
PELHAM BOOKS LTD

Penguin Books Ltd, 27 Wrights Lane, London W8 5TZ
(Publishing & Editorial) and Harmondsworth, Middlesex, England
(Distribution & Warehouse)
Viking Penguin Inc., 40 West 23rd Street, New York, New York 10010, USA.
Penguin Books Australia Ltd, Ringwood, Victoria, Australia.
Penguin Books Canada Limited, 2801 John Street, Markham, Ontario, Canada L3R 1B4
Penguin Books (N.Z.) Ltd, 182–190 Wairau Road, Auckland 10, New Zealand.

British Library Cataloguing in Publication Data
Pot luck: a celebrity cookbook.
1. Cookery, International
641.5   TX725.A1

ISBN 0-7207-1757-4
Typeset by Goodfellow & Egan, Cambridge
Printed and bound by
Arnoldo Mondadori Editore - Verona

◆ Contents ◆

Fish and Shellfish

Meat

Poultry and Game

Puddings and Sweets

◆ *Foreword* ◆
Lord Tonypandy

It is a quarter of a century since I visited Farringtons School for its Speech Day. The memory of that occasion is still vividly in my mind, because I was deeply impressed by the entire tone of the school.

In the intervening years Farringtons has gone from strength to strength. Thousands of girls have been given a solid foundation for life. No formula can measure the influence that this school continues to exercise, both at home and abroad.

I am honoured to be invited to write a foreword for this book of recipes which the school is publishing in support of its effort to raise money for the Save the Children Fund. This is typical of Farringtons' outstanding record of concern for the under-privileged everywhere. I warmly commend this book for your support.

◆ *Introduction* ◆

In 1964 girls of the Lower Sixth at Farringtons School, a Methodist Conference Boarding School for girls at Chislehurst, Kent, found themselves the centre of media attention. Encouraged by their teacher of Religious Studies, Mrs Marjorie Moulton, they began to compile an international cookery book called *Pot Luck*, by writing to celebrities, embassies, and parents (living as far away as Papua New Guinea and Chile, they had exotic food to choose from!), asking them to donate their favourite recipes. The aim was to raise money for the hungry children of the less developed world.

The girls' appearance on BBC Television's 'Town and Around' had a bandwagon effect on the supply of recipes and the demand for the book, which supplied three hundred recipes for five shillings. The first celebrity/charity cookery book of its kind, edited by Judith Carmichael and Kathleen Browne with a huge back-up of girls and staff including Anna Bisset and Nancy Layton, it sold a phenomenal forty-five thousand copies. Miss Frances Wilson, the Headmistress, commented that she would 'long remember the scenes when every ablebodied person seemed to be pressed into service, packing parcels of books, writing invoices, carrying the finished parcels addressed to schools and individuals all over the British Isles and much further afield'.

The book raised £2,300 and helped to buy a mobile nutrition unit for the Freedom from Hunger Campaign and Save the Children Fund. The unit toured Indian Villages, teaching women how to make the most of their resources.

1986 was Farringtons School's seventy-fifth birthday, and a lively Upper Sixth Form, interested in the school's past history, discovered the story of the original *Pot Luck*. Enthusiastic to make a double contribution, to the school for its birthday, and to the starving families of drought-ridden West Africa, they decided to compile another *Pot Luck*. This book owes its creation to the drive and energy of the head girl, Ellen Plant, and her team, who conducted a market research in Bromley, organized every child in the school into writing a letter to the celebrity of her choice, fed the local newspapers with publicity, and worked hard to obtain financial contributions from large firms.

However, at the same time the hugely successful *Food Aid* book was being compiled and the girls felt that it would be sensible to delay *Pot Luck* so that the two books did not compete. In the meantime Ellen left the school and passed the task to Jenny Wright and Helen Chapman. Testing continued in the Home Economics Department under Eira Cuming helped by Anne Button and Christina Yung, and Tim Clough in the Art Department supervised book jacket designs and illustrations.

And here it is at last, with the love of Farringtonians past and present and the willing co-operation of many celebrities from Margaret Thatcher to John Cleese. We hope to outsell the first book, and make a sizeable contribution to the Save the Children Fund. May the luck of our comparative wealth help to fill the pot for the less developed world.

JANET WAYMARK
HEAD OF GEOGRAPHY
FARRINGTONS SCHOOL

◆ *Save the Children* ◆

Today Ramata is a happy healthy child, but it is not long since her mother feared for her life. Luckily help was at hand from a village health worker, newly trained by Save the Children. Without his help Ramata would have died of malnutrition, but his course had taught him to recognize the signs of poor nutrition, as well as to promote health and prevent disease in his remote village in Burkina Faso, West Africa.

When he returned home from his course, the health worker began a survey of all the children in his village to check that they were growing as they should. It was then that he found that Ramata was very weak and under-nourished. Ramata's mother was giving her regular meals of boiled plantain bananas and couldn't understand why her once-lively daughter had lost all zest for life. The health worker explained that Ramata's growing body needed a more varied and nutritious diet and showed her mother how to provide this using cheap local foods. When the Save the Children team re-visited the village a month later, Ramata had quite recovered, with the energy to enjoy each new day.

Overseas

Ramata is just one of millions of children that SCF is helping in over fifty countries.

In the developing world SCF works in two ways: by bringing clinics and feeding schemes to children who need care now, and by setting up long-term programmes to help communities provide better conditions for their children. Often the improvements SCF makes are things we take for granted – like an immunization campaign or a clean water supply. Training for local health workers means that mothers have someone to turn to for treatment and advice, while establishing a village vegetable garden brings better food for all the family.

Save the Children's philosophy is 'Work with the Poorest', so projects are tailored to local conditions and resources. The aim is to meet children's basic needs at a cost which their communities can afford and which governments will eventually be able to take over. Often the best way to help children is to support the whole community: setting up a poultry farm means more than nourishing meals, because any surplus can be sold to bring in much-needed income for a desperately poor village.

In the UK

Even in the mid-1980s there are still many children in the UK living in difficult conditions that can seriously affect their physical, emotional and intellectual growth. SCF has over a hundred projects in the UK, reaching out to more than 10,000 children every day. Work is concentrated in the inner cities, where many children suffer the effects of poverty, unemployment and poor housing.

Save the Children runs family centres, which offer practical help and friendly support for parents as well as activities for their children. These include playgroups for the under-fives and after-school clubs that give older children a lively alternative to street corners and empty houses.

Save the Children also works with young people in trouble with the law, helping them to find a more positive direction for their lives. Other projects include a home for Vietnamese refugee children, a playbus for handicapped and able-bodied children in Glasgow and a youth farm on the outskirts of Belfast. There is support, too, for Traveller children, whose families often find access to health and education services a problem. In the UK, as everywhere it operates, SCF's job is not just to save children, but to give them a life worth living.

◆ *Drinks* ◆

◆ *Quince Wine* ◆

JANET WAYMARK, HEAD OF GEOGRAPHY, FARRINGTONS SCHOOL

This wine, which is sometimes called 'Poor Man's Chateau Y'Quem', is a deep golden colour and has a flavour to match.

About 20 quinces (*Japonica chaenomeles*)
3lb (1.5kg) sugar
Grated rind and juice of 2 lemons

Wine yeast or 1 level teaspoon granulated yeast
1 gallon water
Yeast nutrient

Grate the quinces, cover with water in a saucepan and simmer for 15 minutes. Put the sugar, lemon rind and juice in a large plastic bucket with a lid. Strain the quinces, stir the juice into the mixture in the bucket and leave to cool. Add the yeast and nutrient and leave to stand in a warm place with the lid on for 48 hours. Transfer to a demi-john and fit an air-lock. Leave to ferment, racking (drawing off the sediment) if necessary, for at least a year. Quince wine can ferment for a long time, so it may be advisable to add a campden tablet before bottling.
Makes 1 gallon (4.5 litres)

◆ *Elderflower Champagne* ◆

JOAN LAWRENCE, PLAY GROUP ORGANIZER AND FRIEND OF FARRINGTONS SCHOOL

1 lemon
2 heads elderflowers in full bloom

1½lb (750g) sugar
2 tablespoons white vinegar

Squeeze the juice from the lemon and cut the rind into four pieces. Put juice and rind with the other ingredients in a large plastic bucket. Pour in 1 gallon (4.5 litres) cold water and leave to steep for 2 weeks. The champagne should then be ready to drink.
Makes 1 gallon (4.5 litres)

◆ *Elderflower Wine* ◆

NANCY LAYTON, FORMER HEAD OF MATHEMATICS,
FARRINGTONS SCHOOL

Of all the wines we make, this is the most popular and my personal favourite.

1 pint (600ml) elderflower heads
1 teaspoon yeast compound

1 × 2.24lb (1kg) tin concentrated
    white grape juice
2lb (1kg) sugar, plus extra to taste

Strip the elderflowers from their stalks into a large non-metal bowl. Cover with about 2 pints (1 litre) cold water. Add 1 teaspoon yeast compound to 5fl oz (150ml) warm water (80°F/27°C) in a starter bottle or a ½ pint (300ml) glass. Stir well and cover. Stand in a warm place for a few hours until it is working well, then add to the flowers. Cover with a cloth and leave to stand for 3 days. Strain into a demi-john, add the grape juice and 2lb (1kg) sugar and enough warm water to come within 3in. (7.5cm) of the shoulder of the demi-john. Fit an air-lock and stand in a warm place to ferment. Gently agitate each day until fermentation has subsided. Then add more water until the demi-john is almost full, and leave again until fermentation has finished (there should be no tiny bubbles on the surface). The specific gravity should have fallen to about .996. Add a crushed campden tablet and leave in a cool place until the wine is clear. Taste the wine and add more sugar, 2oz (50g) at a time, to the required sweetness. Add a further campden tablet and bottle when the wine has settled again, taking care not to disturb the sediment. Cork, label and leave in a cool place for at least a year, after which it should be ready to drink.
Makes 1 gallon (4.5 litres)

◆ *Rocks Forge Elderberry Port* ◆

NANCY LAYTON, FORMER HEAD OF MATHEMATICS,
FARRINGTONS SCHOOL

The process starts with a standard elderberry wine, but incorporating a proportion of red grape juice.

For the elderberry wine:
4–6 pints (2.3–3.4 litres)
    elderberries, stripped off their
    stalks
1 × 2.24lb (1kg) tin concentrated
    red grape juice, made up as
    instructed to make 1 gallon (4.5
    litres) wine (usually with 10oz
    (300g) sugar)
4 × 2lb (1kg) bags of sugar

For the port:
Extra sugar

Make the wine mixture up to 5 gallons (22.7 litres) with water. Ferment out in the usual way to make a dry red wine.

When fermentation is complete, or almost so, take as much of this as you wish to make into elderberry port, and put into glass demi-johns with air-locks. To each gallon (4.5 litres) add 4oz (125g) sugar and continue fermentation in a warm place. When fermentation has again ceased, or almost so, and the wine tastes dry, add a further 4oz (125g) and repeat. Then add successive 2oz (50g) increments each time, until the wine will ferment no more. The process can take some months, and when you start you should allow for the tasting at each stage. When the alcohol content is as high as it will go, add a little more sugar to achieve the sweetness you prefer and leave for a few weeks to make sure that no more fermentation is occurring. Add 2 campden tablets per gallon (4.5 litres) and bottle. Mature for at least a year. This year's elderberries make port for the Christmas after next, and, if of a good year, will continue to improve for longer than we have ever managed to wait.

◆ *Damson Gin* ◆

JANET WAYMARK, HEAD OF GEOGRAPHY, FARRINGTONS SCHOOL

Damsons – enough to half-fill a
   bottling jar

4oz (125g) castor sugar
Dry gin

Wash and dry the damsons and prick them with a fork. Put them in a bottling jar with the sugar and fill up with the gin. Replace the ring and lid of the jar and screw down. From time to time, shake the jar until the sugar has dissolved – this will take a few weeks. Leave until Christmas before transferring to small liqueur bottles.

◆ *Hodgkin's Tutti Frutti* ◆

JOAN LAWRENCE, PLAY GROUP ORGANIZER AND FRIEND OF FARRINGTONS SCHOOL

1lb (500g) each of 5 soft fruits:
   small firm strawberries,
   raspberries, cherries and/or
   others in season

1lb (500g) loaf sugar for each 1lb
   (500g) fruit
1 bottle good brandy (1 star)

Put 1lb (500g) strawberries in a stone jar with a tight-fitting lid, add 1lb (500g) loaf sugar, then the bottle of brandy. Put the lid on, cover with a double layer of paper tied down with string and set aside. When raspberries are in season, open the jar *gently*, stir the contents, and add 1lb (500g) raspberries, and a further 1lb (500g) sugar. Tie down again and leave to steep as before. Repeat the process with 1lb (500g) stoned cherries, adding the kernels. Add any other soft fruit of your choice in the same way until you have a total of 5lb (2.25kg) – 1 bottle of brandy will preserve 5lb (2.25kg) fruit. Serve at Christmas in half-filled wine glasses – though this will keep for years if you can bear to leave it!

◆ *Pina Colada* ◆

JULIA TSUI, FARRINGTONS SCHOOL

2fl oz (50ml) light rum
1fl oz (25ml) cream of coconut or
   Malibu

2fl oz (25ml) unsweetened
   pineapple juice
1fl oz (25ml) cream (optional)
Cocktail cherry to garnish

Put all the ingredients except the cherry in a blender with some crushed ice and blend well. Serve garnished with the cherry.
Serves 1

◆ *Rum Swizzle* ◆

JULIA TSUI, FARRINGTONS SCHOOL

1fl oz (25ml) lime juice
1 teaspoon powdered sugar or
   sugar syrup

Soda water
2 dashes bitters
2fl oz (50ml) light rum

Pour the lime juice, sugar and 2fl oz (50ml) soda water into a tall 12fl oz (350ml) glass, add plenty of shaved ice and stir vigorously. Add the bitters and rum, and top up with more soda water. Serve with a swizzle stick in the glass.
Serves 1

◆ *Presbyterian* ◆

JULIA TSUI, FARRINGTONS SCHOOL

2 fl oz (50ml) rye whisky   Club soda
Ginger ale

Pour all the ingredients into an 8fl oz (250ml) highball glass over ice.
Serve with a stirrer.
Serves 1

◆ *Sidecar* ◆

JULIA TSUI, FARRINGTONS SCHOOL

1½fl oz (35ml) brandy
½fl oz (12ml) triple sec or
   Cointreau

Dash of lemon juice
Powdered sugar

Shake the brandy and triple sec or Cointreau together with cracked ice. Frost the rim of a cocktail glass using a little of the lemon juice and the powdered sugar. Pour the remaining lemon juice into the prepared glass and strain the brandy mixture into it.
Serves 1

◆ *Los Angeles* ◆

JULIA TSUI, FARRINGTONS SCHOOL

1½fl oz (35ml) Bourbon
1½fl oz (35ml) lemon or
   pineapple juice
½fl oz (12ml) sweet vermouth

½fl oz sugar syrup (only if using
   lemon juice)
Cocktail cherry to garnish

Shake all the ingredients well together with crushed ice. Strain into an old-fashioned glass over 2 or 3 ice cubes. Serve garnished with the cherry.
Serves 1

◆ *Negroni* ◆

JULIA TSUI, FARRINGTONS SCHOOL

1½fl oz (35ml) dry gin
½fl oz (12ml) Campari bitters
½fl oz (12ml) sweet vermouth

Lemon peel
Dash of soda water

Combine the gin, bitters and vermouth in glass with crushed ice. Add the twisted lemon peel and a dash of soda water. Serve with a stirrer.
Serves 1

◆ *Sangria* ◆

JULIA TSUI, FARRINGTONS SCHOOL

4 oranges
1 bottle Spanish full red wine or
    California Zinfandel

Juice of 1 lemon
3oz (75g) powdered sugar
Soda water

Squeeze the juice from 1 orange and slice the remaining 3. Place all the ingredients except a few of the orange slices in a punch bowl with some ice cubes and stir gently. Add soda water to taste. Float the reserved orange slices on top.
Serves 5 to 8

◆ *Margarita* ◆

JULIA TSUI, FARRINGTONS SCHOOL

1½ fl oz (35ml) tequila
¼ fl oz (6ml) triple sec

Juice of ½ lemon or lime

Prepare a cocktail glass by rubbing the rim with the cut surface of a lemon or lime and spinning the glass upside down in a dish of salt.
  Put all the ingredients in a mixer glass with crushed ice, stir, then strain into the prepared cocktail glass.
Serves 1

◆ *Zombie* ◆

JULIA TSUI, FARRINGTONS SCHOOL

2 fl oz (50ml) light rum
1 fl oz (25ml) Jamaican rum
½ fl oz (12ml) apricot brandy
½ teaspoon powdered sugar
Juice of 1 lime

½ teaspoon unsweetened
  pineapple juice
Sprig of mint and cocktail cherry
  to garnish
½ fl oz (12ml) Demerara rum
  (optional)

Shake all the ingredients well together with cracked ice. Pour unstrained into a 14 fl oz (415ml) glass half-full of cracked ice. Decorate with a sprig of mint and a cherry. Serve with straws. Float ½ fl oz (12ml) Demerara rum on the surface if you wish.
Serves 1

Snacks, Supper Dishes & Sauces

◆ *Macaroni and Cheese* ◆

RONALD REAGAN, PRESIDENT OF THE USA

8oz (250g) macaroni
1 teaspoon butter
1 egg, beaten
1 teaspoon mustard powder

1 teaspoon salt
8fl oz (250ml) milk
6oz (175g) strong cheese, grated

Cook the macaroni in boiling water until tender. Drain thoroughly. Stir in the butter and egg. Mix the mustard and salt with 1 tablespoon hot water and add to the milk. Add the cheese, reserving some to sprinkle on top of the finished dish. Put the macaroni into a buttered casserole, add the milk mixture and stir well. Sprinkle with the reserved cheese. Bake in the oven at gas mark 4, 350°F (180°C) for about 45 minutes or until the custard is set and the top is crusty.
Serves 2

◆ *Summer Lunch* ◆

DAME PEGGY ASHCROFT, ACTRESS

4 eggs
Butter
Smoked salmon or tinned
   anchovy fillets, cut into small
   pieces

1 × 15oz (425g) tin Crosse and
   Blackwell's consommé, chilled
Chopped parsley

Scramble the eggs in the butter, put them in a deep dish and allow to cool. Scatter the pieces of smoked salmon or anchovy over the top. Remove the jellied consommé from the tin and chop. Place it on top of the scrambled eggs and cover with a thick layer of chopped parsley.
Serves 2

◆ *Yorkshire Pudding* ◆

ROWAN ATKINSON, COMEDIAN

This recipe, served in the traditional way separately before the main course, I have got to work only once; the reason being that it is based on a suck-it-and-see formula of my mother's which has never been written down.

12 heaped dessertspoons plain flour	Salt and pepper
2 eggs	About 5fl oz (150ml) milk
	Beef dripping or lard

Pre-heat the oven to gas mark 9, 475°F (240°C).

Put the flour into a bowl. Make a hollow in the centre and break the eggs into it. Add a good sprinkling of salt and pepper and the milk. Beat it all together thoroughly with a fork or spoon, perhaps adding a little water to ensure that it is smooth.

Heat ¼in (6mm) of beef dripping or lard in a baking tin to as high a temperature as possible, then pour the mixture into it, perhaps keeping a little back to thicken the gravy of the main course. Bake in the oven for about 10 minutes, then reduce the heat to gas mark 7, 425°F (220°C) and continue to bake for a further 15 to 20 minutes. The mixture should rise: leave until a good brown colour.

Serves 2 to 4

◆ *Emmentaler Fondue* ◆

WEST GERMAN EMBASSY

2 cloves of garlic, halved
12oz (350g) Allgau Emmentaler
    cheese, grated
5fl oz (150ml) milk
15fl oz (450ml) German white
    wine

1 tablespoon Kirsch
Salt and pepper
1 large loaf of bread, cut into 1in.
    (2.5cm) cubes, to serve

Rub the cut sides of the garlic cloves around the sides and bottom of a fondue pot. Put the cheese and milk in the pot and cook over a very low heat, stirring, until the cheese melts. Gradually stir in the wine and Kirsch and season to taste with salt and pepper. Serve with the cubes of bread, which are dipped into the cheese fondue.
Serves 4

◆ *Toasted Cheese* ◆

LADY CARRINGTON, WIFE OF LORD CARRINGTON,
SECRETARY GENERAL OF NATO

3oz (75g) butter
8oz (250g) dry farmhouse
    Cheddar cheese, grated

8 tablepoons cream
3 size 3 egg yolks
Salt, pepper and cayenne

Melt the butter in a pan over a low heat, add the remaining ingredients and stir them vigorously together. Heat gently, continuing to stir, until the mixture thickens to a cream-like consistency. Do not allow it to boil: be patient. Divide between 8 ramekins and brown lightly under the grill. Serve with plenty of toast fingers, or pieces of freshly baked bread.
Serves 8

◆ *Golden Flan* ◆

WENDY CRAIG, ACTRESS

8oz (250g) shortcrust pastry with 2oz (50g) finely grated mature Cheddar cheese added to the rubbed-in mixture before it is mixed to a dough

1 × 10½oz (300g) tin creamed sweetcorn
3 eggs, lightly beaten
3oz (75g) carrots, grated
4oz (125g) Cheddar cheese, grated
Salt and freshly ground pepper

Pre-heat oven to gas mark 6, 400°F (200°C).

Line a 9in. (23cm) flan tin with the cheese pastry and bake blind in the oven for about 15 minutes. Reduce the oven temperature to gas mark 4, 350°F (180°C) in preparation for cooking the filled flan.

While the pastry case is cooking, make the filling. Mix together the sweetcorn, eggs, carrots and cheese, season well with salt and pepper and pour into the flan case. Bake in the oven for 30 to 40 minutes or until set and golden brown.

Serves 6

◆ *Grothies Groovy Russian Eggs* ◆

'SPLASH', THAMES TELEVISION

4 hard-boiled eggs
1 tablespoon vinegar
1 tablespoon olive oil

1 teaspoon mustard
Salt and pepper to taste

When the eggs are cool, take the shells off and halve them. Remove the yolks carefully in one piece. Mix all the other ingredients together thoroughly and pour a little into the hollow in each egg white. Then replace the yolks.

Serves 2

◆ *Welsh Rarebit Plus Cackleberrieg and Juglans Regia* ◆

DAVID BELLAMY, NATURALIST

2 slices wholemeal bread
Mature Cheddar cheese, grated
Cayenne pepper

2 free-range eggs
2 slices pickled walnut (optional)

Toast the bread lightly on one side only. Place the grated cheese on the untoasted side, sprinkle with cayenne pepper and grill slowly until the cheese is melted and bubbling.

Meanwhile, poach the eggs and place one on top of each slice of cheese on toast. Serve straight away with a slice of pickled walnut on each egg if you wish.

Serves 2

◆ *Bacon, Cheese and Marmite Sandwiches* ◆

STEVE DAVIS, SNOOKER PLAYER

Bacon rashers
Butter
2 slices brown bread

Cheddar cheese, sliced
Marmite

Grill the bacon. Meanwhile, butter both slices of bread and spread *one* buttered slice only with Marmite. Cover the Marmite with slices of cheese, then top with the sizzling bacon rashers. Place the second slice of bread on the top. Cut into quarters and serve immediately with a nice cup of tea (no sugar!)

Serves 1

◆ *Crispy Stuffed Tomatoes* ◆
WEST GERMAN EMBASSY

1 green-skinned eating apple,
  cored and diced
2 teaspoons lemon juice
3 frankfurters
1 small onion, finely chopped
3 German pickled gherkins,
  chopped

3oz (75g) Tilsiter cheese, diced
2–3 teaspoons German egg
  mayonnaise
Salt and pepper
8 large tomatoes
Lettuce leaves, parsley sprigs

Combine the apple and lemon juice. Dice 2 of the frankfurters and add to the apple with the onion, gherkins and cheese. Mix well, add sufficient mayonnaise to bind, and season to taste with salt and pepper.

Cut the tops off the tomatoes, and scoop out and discard the seeds. Fill the tomato shells with the prepared mixture. Slice the remaining frankfurter and arrange on top of the tomatoes. Serve the tomatoes on a bed of lettuce, garnished with parsley.
Serves 4

◆ *Oatmeal Crumbs* ◆

SANDY GALL, NEWSCASTER

This well-known Scottish recipe is an alternative accompaniment to roast chicken – tastier than stuffing.

Coarsely ground oatmeal
Vegetable oil or butter for frying

Heat the oil or butter in a frying pan over a low flame. Add the oatmeal and stir for several minutes until lightly browned. Serve separately.

◆ *Rose Petal Vinegar* ◆

EIRA CUMING, HEAD OF HOME ECONOMICS, FARRINGTONS SCHOOL

Rose petals
White wine vinegar

Fill a jar with rose petals, press down well and cover with white wine vinegar. Leave for a month, then strain. Use in salad dressings.

◆ *Peanut Sauce* ◆

SUE LAWLEY, TELEVISION JOURNALIST

½oz (15g) margarine
½ small onion, finely chopped
1 small clove of garlic, finely
    chopped
1 dessertspoon soy sauce

3 tablespoons crunchy peanut
    butter
4 tablespoons single cream
1 teaspoon lemon juice

Heat the margarine in a small pan and fry the onion and garlic for 5 minutes. Stir in the soy sauce and peanut butter and mix well. Let this mixture cool; then, when ready to serve, stir in the cream and lemon juice.
Serves 4

◆ *Deep-fried Camembert* ◆

WEST GERMAN EMBASSY

4 halves German Camembert
    cheese
Coarsely ground black pepper
Breadcrumbs for coating

2 eggs, beaten
8 tablespoons gooseberry
    conserve
Vegetable oil for deep-frying

Cut the Camembert halves in two and refrigerate for at least 1 hour. Mix together the black pepper and the breadcrumbs. Dip the chilled Camembert pieces in the beaten egg and then into the breadcrumb mixture. Return the crumbed Camembert pieces to the refrigerator for 10 minutes. Meanwhile, put the gooseberry conserve in a small bowl and heat through over a pan of simmering water. Heat the oil to 350°F (180°C) and deep-fry the Camembert pieces until golden brown. Drain and serve immediately with the warmed gooseberry conserve poured over.
Serves 4

·Starters·

◆ *Carrot and Orange Soup* ◆

RT HON DENIS HEALEY, MP

12oz (350g) carrots, sliced
2 medium onions, chopped
1½oz (40g) butter

1½ pints (850ml) stock
1 bayleaf
2 large oranges

Sweat the carrots and onions in the butter until the onion is transparent. Add the stock, bayleaf and the grated rind of 1 orange. Simmer until the vegetables are tender. Remove the bayleaf and liquidize the soup, or rub through a sieve. Pour in the juice of both oranges and re-heat to serve, or serve chilled.

Serves 4

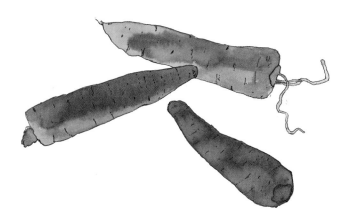

◆ *French Onion Soup* ◆

RT HON EDWARD HEATH, MP

Knob of butter
4 large or 6 medium onions,
    thickly sliced
2 pints (1 litre) stock

Salt and pepper
4 slices of bread, toasted
4oz (125g) cheese, grated

Heat the butter in a large heavy saucepan and fry the onions over a moderate heat until golden brown – stir from time to time to prevent sticking and take great care not to burn them. Pour in the stock, bring to the boil and simmer for 30 to 45 minutes with the lid on. Add salt and pepper to taste.

   Serve in four individual bowls, floating a slice of toast on each serving. Sprinkle generously with the grated cheese.

   This is a meal in itself.

Serves 4

◆ *Simple Soup* ◆

RICHARD BAKER, BROADCASTER

This was one of the late Joyce Grenfell's recipes.

1 large potato, diced
1 large onion, diced
1 clove of garlic, chopped
A little vegetable oil
2 pints (1 litre) chicken stock

Salt and pepper
6 medium tomatoes, peeled and
    quartered
Chopped fresh or dried mint to
    taste

Gently fry the potato, onion and garlic in the oil until the onion is transparent. Add the stock and simmer until the vegetables are tender. Season to taste with salt and pepper. Add the tomatoes and blend well with the cooked mixture. Add lots of mint. Serve the soup hot or cold.

Serves 4 to 6

◆ *Summer Vegetable Soup with Frankfurters* ◆

WEST GERMAN EMBASSY

2 pints (1 litre) beef stock
4oz (125g) carrots, diced
4oz (125g) peas (shelled weight)
4oz (125g) celery, chopped
8oz (250g) potatoes, diced
4oz (125g) courgettes, sliced

¼ medium cauliflower, broken
   into small florets
2 small tomatoes, chopped
1 small onion, chopped
Salt and pepper
4 frankfurters, thinly sliced

Bring the stock to the boil in a large covered saucepan, add all the vegetables and simmer for 30 to 35 minutes. Season to taste with salt and pepper. Add the frankfurters to the soup and continue to simmer until they are just heated through. Serve with crusty bread.
Serves 4 to 6

◆ *Cream of Parsnip Soup* ◆

LONDON HILTON HOTEL

1lb (500g) parsnips
3oz (75g) potatoes
2oz (50g) onion
2oz (50g) celery
2oz (50g) leek

2oz (50g) butter
2 pints (1 litre) chicken stock
8fl oz (250ml) single cream
Salt and pepper
Chopped parsley to garnish

Prepare all the vegetables and slice thinly. Sauté them lightly in the butter for a few minutes, then add the chicken stock and simmer until they are tender. Place the soup in a liquidizer goblet and blend until smooth. Stir in the cream and season to taste with salt and pepper. Sprinkle with chopped parsley before serving.
Serves 6

◆ *Consommé Pettifer* ◆

ESTHER RANTZEN, TELEVISION
PERSONALITY AND CAMPAIGNER

This recipe may not be cheap, but it tastes delicious – and it is not exactly time-consuming.

2 × 15oz (425g) tins consommé
2½fl oz (60ml) double cream

1 × 2oz (50g) jar mock caviare
   (lumpfish roe)
1 lemon, sliced

Chill the tins of consommé thoroughly in the refrigerator until jellied. Remove the consommé from the tins and chop. Whip the cream until it thickens enough to stand in soft peaks. Divide the consommé between four bowls and put a dollop of cream on top of each. Sprinkle mock caviare on the cream. Hang a slice of fresh lemon on the rim of each bowl to serve.
Serves 4

◆ *Emmentaler Soup* ◆

WEST GERMAN EMBASSY

1oz (25g) German butter
1 small carrot, grated
1 small onion, grated
1 stick celery, finely chopped
1 teaspoon mild German mustard
1½ pints (850ml) chicken stock

5fl oz (150ml) milk
6oz (175g) Allgau Emmentaler
   cheese, grated
Salt and pepper
2–3 tablespoons quark (low-fat
   soft cheese) – optional

Heat the butter in a large saucepan and fry the carrot, onion and celery until very soft. Add the mustard and stock and bring to the boil. Add the milk and cheese and continue to heat while stirring until the cheese is melted. Season to taste with salt and pepper.

You can thicken the soup if you wish by adding 2 or 3 tablespoons of quark, but allow it to cool a little first.
Serves 4

◆ *Mackerel Pâté* ◆

EIRA CUMING, HEAD OF HOME ECONOMICS, FARRINGTONS
SCHOOL

2 smoked mackerel fillets
3½oz (100g) butter, melted
Finely grated rind of 1 lemon

2 tablespoons whipped double
  cream
Freshly ground black pepper

Remove the skin from the mackerel fillets and flake the flesh, making
sure that no bones remain. Put the flaked fish into a food processor or
blender and blend well. Pour in the melted butter, add the lemon rind
and blend again. Fold in the whipped cream and season to taste with
black pepper. Chill before serving with hot toast.
Serves 4

◆ *Black Olive Pâté* ◆

SIR LINDSAY RING, FORMER LORD MAYOR OF LONDON AND
FARRINGTONS SCHOOL EX-GOVERNOR

4oz (125g) unsalted butter
1 medium onion, finely chopped
10–12oz (300–350g) black olives,
  drained, rinsed and stoned

3 tablespoons cream cheese
Pinch of dried thyme
Black pepper

Heat a small knob of butter in a pan and sauté the onion in it until very
soft. Mix together the onion, olives, cream cheese and the rest of the
butter and add thyme and black pepper to taste. (You will not need to
add any salt as there is plenty in the olives.) Place the mixture in the
goblet of a liquidizer and blend well. Chill before serving.
Serves 4

◆ *Luxury Liver Pâté* ◆
WEST GERMAN EMBASSY

11oz (325g) German smooth liver
   sausage, skin removed
2oz (50g) German butter, melted
2 tablespoons German Brandy
¼ teaspoon garlic salt

Freshly milled white or black
   pepper
Lettuce leaves or cress, and black
   olives to garnish

Place the liver sausage in a bowl and add the butter, brandy, garlic salt
and pepper. Beat until smooth. Line a serving plate with lettuce leaves
or cress and, using a forcing bag and meringue nozzle, pipe the pâté into
a decorative mound on top of the greenery. Garnish with black olives
and chill lightly before serving. Serve with fingers of hot toast.
Serves 4

◆ *Egg Mousse* ◆
TONY HART, CARTOONIST

1 tablespoon chicken stock (made
   with a cube if you wish)
1 teaspoon powdered gelatine
3 hard-boiled eggs

1 raw egg
4fl oz (125ml) vegetable oil
Pinch of curry powder (optional)

Heat the stock (but do not boil), sprinkle the gelatine into it and stir until
dissolved. Place in a liquidizer goblet with all the other ingredients and
blend until smooth. Pour into a bowl or mould and chill thoroughly until
set.

   This goes well with crispbread, and is delicious served with smoked
salmon.
Serves 3 to 4

◆ *Terrine de Legumes Délices Potager en Arc en Ciel* ◆

MARJAN LOSNIK, CLARIDGE'S HOTEL

For the terrine:
4oz (125g) broccoli purée
4oz (125g) leek purée
8oz (250g) turnip purée
8oz (250g) carrot purée
8oz (250g) artichoke purée
8oz (250g) red pepper purée

6 egg yolks
4fl oz (250ml) milk
Salt
Pepper
1 sachet powdered gelatine
10fl oz (300g) double cream

Mix the broccoli and leek purées together.

Put the egg yolks into a basin set over a pan of simmering water and whisk until thickened. Heat the milk and whisk into the egg yolks, and add salt and pepper to taste. Dissolve the gelatine in hot water and add to the egg and milk mixture. Remove from the heat and continue whisking to cool a little. Whip the cream until it stands in soft peaks and fold into the mixture. Divide the mixture into four equal parts and add one to each of the vegetable purées. Adjust the seasoning.

Put the vegetable purées in layers in a well-chilled terrine, starting with the turnip purée, followed by the carrot, artichoke, broccoli/leek and the red pepper purée. Allow each purée to set thoroughly in the refrigerator before you add the next – it will take about 4 hours to complete the terrine.

Serve with tomato and basil coulis (purée).
Serves 8 to 10

◆ *Crème à la Markova* ◆

DAME ALICIA MARKOVA, FORMER PRIMA BALLERINA

1 × 4 fl oz (125ml) tin or bottle
   tomato juice

French vermouth to taste
Soured cream to serve

Put the tomato juice and vermouth in a pan and bring gently to boiling point. Remove from the heat and add a spoonful of soured cream before serving.
Serves 1

◆ *Melon à la Robert* ◆

JOHN INMAN, COMEDIAN

1 Ogen melon
2 oz (50g) smoked salmon

Prawn cocktail sauce to taste

Cut the melon in half and remove the flesh, reserving the shells. Dice the flesh. Cut the smoked salmon into small squares and mix with the diced melon flesh and prawn cocktail sauce to taste. Place in the melon shells and chill before serving.
Serves 2

◆ *Cucumber Starter* ◆

COSTAS ONISIFOROU, BAKER AND FRIEND OF FARRINGTONS SCHOOL

1 medium-sized cucumber, diced
2 × 5 fl oz (150ml) cartons natural
   yogurt
½ clove of garlic, chopped and
   crushed

Fresh mint, chopped, and a little
   olive oil to garnish

Mix the cucumber, yogurt and garlic and chill in the refrigerator for 1 hour. Sprinkle with chopped mint and oil to taste, and serve with French bread.
Serves 4

◆ *Vegetable* & *Salad Dishes* ◆

◆ *Baked Potatoes with Swedish Red Caviare and Soured Cream* ◆

SWEDISH EMBASSY

8 large baking potatoes, well
   scrubbed
Spring onions or chives, finely
   chopped, to taste

10fl oz (300ml) soured cream
3½oz (100g) Swedish red caviare
   (bleak roe)

Pre-heat the oven to gas mark 7, 425°F (220°C).

Place the potatoes on an ovenproof plate or in a roasting tin. Bake in the oven for 45 minutes to 1 hour, or until cooked through. Meanwhile, stir the spring onions or chives into the soured cream.

Remove the cooked potatoes from the oven, cut a cross in the top of each and squeeze up a little of the contents. Spoon some soured cream into the centre and top with caviare. Hand the rest of the soured cream separately.

Serves 8

◆ *Jim's Tatties* ◆

JIM DAVIDSON, ACTOR

1 egg, beaten
A little milk
Salt and pepper
A little flour

1 large potato, peeled and grated
Vegetable oil or lard for shallow-
   frying

Beat together the egg, milk, pepper and salt. Stir in the flour and the grated potato. Heat the oil or lard in a frying pan and spoon in the potato mixture. Fry until golden brown; turn and do the other side. The result should resemble a kind of pancake.

Serves 1

◆ *Herb Brie-stuffed Jacket Potatoes* ◆

GERMAN EMBASSY

4 baked potatoes
3 oz (75g) herb Brie, de-rinded
½ teaspoon salt

1 egg yolk
2oz (50g) German butter,
  softened

Pre-heat the oven to gas mark 5, 375°F (190°C).
   Slice the top off each potato and carefully remove the flesh. Beat together the potato flesh, herb Brie, salt, egg yolk and butter until well mixed. Return the mixture to the potato skins. Place on a baking sheet and bake in the oven for 10 minutes until the filling is golden brown.
Serves 4

◆ *Tomato Pie* ◆

BILLY CONNOLLY, COMEDIAN

Slices of bread
6 eggs
1 pint (600ml) double cream
Tomatoes, sliced
Salt and pepper

For the herb butter:
2oz (50g) butter, softened
1 tablespoon chopped chives
1 tablespoon chopped parsley
1 tablespoon chopped basil

Pre-heat the oven to gas mark 4, 350°F (180°C).
   To make the herb butter, beat the herbs into the butter until well mixed. Spread the herb butter on the bread. Line a greased deep pie dish with the buttered bread.
   Whisk the eggs together, add the cream and set aside.
   Arrange a layer of tomato slices on top of the bread and season well with salt and pepper. Pour on the egg and cream mixture and bake in the oven for 40 minutes or until set and golden brown.
Serves 4

◆ *Veggie Burgers* ◆

WENDY BRUSHNEEN, FARRINGTONS SCHOOL PUPIL

1lb (500g) mashed potatoes or
  cooked rice
2 carrots, grated
Left-over cooked vegetables:
  peas, celery, cauliflower, etc.
Vegetable oil

4oz (125g) unsalted peanuts,
  chopped
Salt and pepper
Beaten egg and breadcrumbs to
  coat

Pre-heat the oven to gas mark 4, 350°F (180°C).

Mix the mashed potatoes or rice with the carrots and cooked vegetables. If the mixture is a little dry, add a few drops of vegetable oil to bind. Add the peanuts and salt and pepper to taste, then work the mixture together so that it has a minced beef-ish texture. Form into burger shapes, brush lightly with beaten egg and roll in breadcrumbs. Place on a greased baking sheet and bake in the oven for 30 minutes.
Makes 6 to 8 burgers

Anchovy and Green Pepper Salad

JULIET PLANT, FARRINGTONS SCHOOL PARENT AND GOVERNOR'S WIFE

3 green peppers
1 × 2oz (50g) tin anchovy fillets

Black pepper

Place the green peppers under a hot grill and turn regularly until they are thoroughly cooked (but not burnt) on all sides. Allow to cool, then peel, cut out the stalk and core, and remove the seeds. Slice the flesh into strips.

Mix the anchovy fillets, including their oil, with the strips of green pepper. Season to taste with black pepper.

This salad can be made in advance and refrigerated to serve the next day. It is delicious as an hors d'oeuvre.

Serves 4

Green Bean and Bacon Salad

JULIET PLANT, FARRINGTONS SCHOOL PARENT AND
GOVERNOR'S WIFE

1lb (500g) green beans (string
   beans are best)
2 thick rashers of bacon, diced

3 tablespoons vinaigrette
   dressing
Nutmeg

Prepare the beans and cook in lightly salted simmering water. When they are cooked, drain them but leave them in the covered pan to keep warm.

Meanwhile fry the bacon in a frying pan – you should not need to add any fat as it will make its own. Add the hot bacon and vinaigrette dressing to the beans while they are still warm and mix lightly. Turn the mixture into serving dish and add grated nutmeg to taste.

Cooked ham may be used instead of bacon to make a more delicate-flavoured dish.

Serves 4

·Fish & Shellfish·

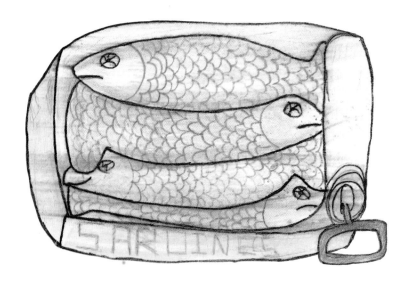

◆ *Tuna Crêpe Cake* ◆

ANITA DOBSON OF *EASTENDERS*

8 cooked crêpes
1 × 15oz (425g) tin tuna, drained
   and flaked
10fl oz (300ml) white sauce

2 spring onions, chopped
2 hard-boiled eggs, chopped
1 tablespoon chopped parsley

Pre-heat the oven to gas mark 5, 375°F (190°C).

The crêpes and white sauce must be hot before you start to assemble the dish. Mix together the tuna, white sauce, spring onions, hard-boiled eggs and parsley. Lay a crêpe flat on a greased ovenproof serving dish. Cover with a little of the tuna mixture, then put another crêpe on top. Continue making layers in this way, ending with a crêpe. Cover the cake with foil and re-heat in the oven for 15 minutes. Serve hot.
Serves 4

◆ *Easy Salmon or Tuna Mousse* ◆

SARAH LOVETT-SMITH, FARRINGTONS SCHOOL PUPIL

1 × 6oz (175g) tin evaporated
   milk
1oz (25g) powdered gelatine
1 × 7oz (200g) tin salmon or tuna,
   drained and flaked

1 × 7oz (200g) jar sandwich
   spread
1 tablespoon mayonnaise
Salt, pepper and vinegar

Whisk the evaporated milk until thick. Dissolve the gelatine in 2 to 3 tablespoons water. Mix the fish, sandwich spread and mayonnaise, add the gelatine, season to taste with salt, pepper and a little vinegar, and fold in the evaporated milk. Pour the mixture into an oiled mould and leave to set in the refrigerator for at least 3 to 4 hours.
Serves 4

◆ *Salmon Puffs* ◆

SARAH GARRETT, FARRINGTONS SCHOOL PUPIL

1 × 7oz (200g) tin red salmon,
  drained
2 eggs, separated
1oz (25g) plain flour

½ teaspoon salt
Freshly ground black pepper
Vegetable oil for deep-frying

Remove the bones and skin from the salmon and flake the flesh with a fork. Beat the egg yolks until creamy and stir into the salmon with the flour and seasoning to taste. Whisk the egg whites until stiff but not dry and fold into the salmon mixture.

Drop spoonfuls of the mixture into hot oil and deep-fry, turning once, until a golden colour. Drain on kitchen paper. Serve immediately with potatoes and peas or green beans – the puffs will not keep.
Serves 2

◆ *Haddock Crumble* ◆

SARAH GARRETT, FARRINGTONS SCHOOL PUPIL

1½–2lb (750g–1kg) haddock
  fillet, skinned
1 small onion, chopped
Juice of 1½ lemons
Salt and freshly milled black
  pepper

4oz (125g) breadcrumbs
2oz cheese, grated
Chopped parsley
1oz (25g) butter, melted

Pre-heat the oven to gas mark 4, 350°F (180°C).

Place the fish in an ovenproof dish, add the onion and pour over the lemon juice. Add salt and pepper to taste and 3 to 4 tablespoons cold water.

Combine the breadcrumbs with the cheese, parsley and a little salt and pepper. Stir in the melted butter.

Spread the breadcrumb mixture evenly over the fish and bake in the oven for 45 minutes. Serve with a green or mixed salad.

◆ *Trout with Caper Sauce* ◆

LESLIE GRANTHAM OF *EASTENDERS*

5 tablespoons vegetable oil
1 large clove of garlic, crushed
Juice of 1 large lemon
4oz (125g) capers, drained and
   coarsely chopped

Salt and freshly milled black
   pepper
2 trout, gutted

A few hours before the cooking time, put the oil in a glass or earthenware bowl with the crushed garlic and beat in the lemon juice followed by the capers, salt and pepper. Leave aside for the flavour to develop.

When you are ready to cook, remove the grill rack and line the grill pan with foil. Pre-heat the grill and arrange the fish on the foil. Gash each side of the fish twice on the thickest part of the body. Brush a little oil on both sides. Sprinkle with salt and pepper and pour over the caper sauce. Grill under a high heat so that the trout skins turn crisply brown – this will take 3 to 4 minutes on each side. Serve with the cooking juices poured over.

Serves 2

◆ Sole St Clement ◆

LORD SOPER, METHODIST PREACHER

8 fillets of sole, skinned and rolled
10fl oz (300ml) milk
1oz (25g) butter
1oz (25g) flour
Salt and pepper

Grated rind and juice of ½ lemon
    and ½ orange
10fl oz (300ml) natural yogurt
10fl oz (300ml) soured cream
Brown breadcrumbs

Poach the fish lightly in the milk. Strain and reserve the milk to make a thick cheese sauce: melt the butter, mix in the flour, then gradually add the milk, stirring all the time, until the sauce thickens. Season to taste with salt and pepper.

Heat the oven to gas mark 2, 300°F (150°C).

Put the fish in a large shallow baking dish. Pour over the orange and lemon juice. Mix together the yogurt, soured cream and cheese sauce and pour this over the fish. Sprinkle with the breadcrumbs. Cook on the top shelf of the oven until heated through. If necessary, brown for a few seconds under a hot grill. Serve decorated with a little grated orange and lemon rind.
Serves 4

◆ Grilled King-size Prawns ◆

CHARLES DANCE, ACTOR

3oz (75g) butter melted
Best-quality olive oil
Finely grated rind and juice of 2
    lemons

1 clove of garlic, crushed
Salt and black pepper
As many king-size prawns as 2
    people can eat or afford

In a glass or earthenware bowl, mix the melted butter with a couple of tablespoons of oil, the lemon rind and juice, the garlic and salt and pepper to taste. Add the prawns and marinate for an hour or so, turning occasionally.

Remove the rack from the grill pan and line the pan with aluminium foil. Pre-heat the grill. Put the prawns and their marinade into the pan and grill for a few minutes on each side, turning from time to time and basting with the marinade.

Serves 2

◆ *Prawns and Sweetcorn* ◆

SARAH LOVETT-SMITH, FARRINGTONS SCHOOL PUPIL

Spring onions, finely chopped
Rosemary, crushed
Butter or vegetable oil
4–6oz (125–175g) frozen prawns,
   thawed and patted dry

1 × 10oz (300g) tin sweetcorn,
   drained
Black pepper

Fry the spring onions lightly with rosemary to taste in the butter or oil. Add the prawns and sweetcorn and heat through. Season with black pepper. Serve as a starter with crisp French bread.

◆ *Sweet and Sour Herrings* ◆

MAUREEN LIPMAN, ACTRESS

8 herrings, gutted
1 large onion, sliced into rings
6 tablespoons brown sugar (or to
  taste)

Black peppercorns
Malt vinegar

Pre-heat the oven to gas mark 1, 275°F (140°C).

Fillet the herrings and split the fillets straight down the middle so that you have 16 pieces of fish. Roll each piece carefully and secure with a cocktail stick. Place the herring rolls in a lidded casserole just big enough to take them all side by side in a single layer. Cover with onion rings. Sprinkle over the sugar and throw in some black peppercorns. Nearly cover this mixture with equal parts of water and malt vinegar and put the lid on the casserole. Cook in the oven for about 1½ hours or until the flesh of the fish flakes.

After about 1 hour of the cooking time, remove from the oven and taste the liquid. If too sweet for your taste, add a little more vinegar. If too tart, add a little more sugar. The ideal for this dish is slightly tart, rather than slightly sweet. Return the casserole to the oven without the lid for the rest of the cooking time until the herrings and onions are slightly brown and crisp – the bits showing, that is.

When cooked, remove from the oven and allow to cool before placing in the refrigerator. This dish is delicious cold, and will keep for up to three days if refrigerated.

Serves 8

◆ *Ceviche* ◆

NORMAN RICHARDSON, FORMER MAYOR OF DURHAM

1lb (500g) very fresh halibut
Juice of 2 large lemons (about 6
　tablespoons)
1 onion, chopped
8oz (250g) tomatoes, peeled (see
　page 91), de-seeded and
　coarsely chopped

1 green pepper, de-seeded and
　chopped
1 tablespoon chopped parsley
1 tablespoon olive oil
4 tablespoons vinegar
Salt and freshly milled pepper
Dash of Tabasco sauce

Trim the fish, remove the skin, and cut into small neat pieces. Place in a
glass or earthenware bowl and pour over the strained lemon juice. Place
in the refrigerator and leave to marinate for 4 to 6 hours, turning the fish
from time to time.

Add the onion, tomatoes, green pepper and parsley to the fish with
the oil and vinegar, a seasoning of salt and pepper and a dash of Tabasco
sauce. Continue to marinate for several hours more, then check the
seasoning and flavour before serving.
Serves 4

◆ *Gravad Lax from Sweden* ◆

SWEDISH EMBASSY

1 salmon
4 tablespoons sugar
4 tablespoons salt

2 teaspoons white peppercorns,
    crushed
Fresh dill

Fillet about 3lb (1.5kg) salmon from the middle part of the fish. Remove all the small bones but not the skin.

Mix the sugar, salt and peppercorns together. Rub the salmon fillets with most of this mixture, reserving a little.

Place a layer of dill at the bottom of a shallow dish and then put a salmon fillet on top, skin side downwards. Cover with a generous layer of dill. Sprinkle with the remainder of the spice mixture. Place the other salmon fillet on top, skin side upwards, so that the thin part rests on the thicker end of the lower piece. Cover with a generous layer of dill.

Place a very light weight on top (the juices must not be pressed out of the salmon). Refrigerate for 1 or 2 days, turning the salmon over half-way through.

To serve, scrape off the dill and spices. Cut into slices and serve with cold Gravlax Sauce, lemon wedges and boiled potatoes.
Allow approx 4oz (125g) per person

◆ *Gravlax Sauce* ◆

SWEDISH EMBASSY

2 tablespoons mustard
1 tablespoon sugar
1 tablespoon vinegar

6 tablespoons oil
6 tablespoons soured cream
Fresh dill, finely chopped

Mix the mustard, sugar and vinegar together in a bowl. Add the oil gradually until well blended, stirring vigorously. Finally, add the cream and plenty of dill.

Serve with Gravad Lax.

·Meat·

◆ *Fruity Lamb with Rice* ◆

ELIZABETH WALLACE,
FARRINGTONS SCHOOL EX-GOVERNOR

3lb (1.5kg) neck fillet of lamb
2 tablespoons oil
Salt and freshly ground black
    pepper
2 teaspoons garam masala
1 teaspoon ground cinnamon
1 teaspoon mustard seed
2oz (50g) raisins

4oz (125g) dried apricots, halved
4 oz (125g) dried figs, halved
8oz (250g) brown rice, well
    washed
2 pints (1 litre) light stock or water
1 head of celery, stalks trimmed
    and sliced and leaves roughly
    chopped

Pre-heat the oven to gas mark 2, 300°F (150°C).

Brown the lamb in the hot oil in a flameproof casserole. Drain off the
excess fat. Add the seasoning, spices and dried fruits, and rice, stirring
well. Bring the stock or water to the boil in a separate pan and pour over
the meat. Cover and cook in the oven for 1 hour. Then stir in the sliced
celery stalks and adjust the seasoning. Return to the oven for a final 10
minutes, or until the rice is cooked. Serve garnished with the chopped
celery leaves.
Serves 6

◆ *An Uncle's Concoction* ◆

LORD TAYLOR OF HADFIELD,
FOUNDER TAYLOR WOODROW GROUP

Very unusual and very delicious!

1 cow-heel
1lb (500g) lamb tenderloin,
  cubed
2 × 15oz (425g) tins butter beans

1 × 14oz (400g) tin peas
1lb (500g) carrots, thickly sliced
Butter

Pre-heat the oven to gas mark 3, 325°F (170°C).
   Put all the ingredients in a casserole with a little butter and cook slowly and steadily in the oven for about 2½ to 3 hours.
Serves 4 to 6

◆ *Rump Steaks with Spicy Mustard* ◆ *Sauce*

WEST GERMAN EMBASSY

4 rump steaks
5 tablespoons quark (low-fat soft
  cheese)
2 tablespoons wine vinegar

1 teaspoon Dusseldorf mustard
1 teaspoon chopped parsley
Salt and pepper
1 teaspoon Worcestershire sauce

Grill or fry the steaks to taste. Combine all the other ingredients in a bowl. Serve the steaks immediately, topped with the sauce.
   This sauce is also delicious on jacket potatoes.
Serves 4

❖ *Steak Diane* ❖

TERRY VENABLES, FOOTBALL MANAGER AND
EX-FARRINGTONS SCHOOL PARENT

1 thick slice fillet steak
Salt and freshly ground pepper
2–3oz (50–75g) butter
2 tablespoons finely chopped
  parsley
1 clove of garlic, finely chopped

2 tablespoons chopped chives
  (optional)
1 tablespoon Worcestershire
  sauce
1 tablespoon brandy

Remove all the fat and gristle from the steak, then slice almost through horizontally and open out like butterfly wings. Place the steak between two pieces of greaseproof paper and flatten out with a steak mallet or rolling pin so it looks like a large pancake – no thicker than ¼in. (6mm). Sprinkle lightly with salt and pepper.

Heat the butter in a heavy frying pan and, when it is sizzling, drop in the steak. Shake the pan by the handle to prevent the steak from sticking. Fry for 40 seconds on the underside for rare steak, 1 minute for medium. Keep the heat high enough for the steak to brown quickly and, if necessary, add a little more butter. Turn the steak over after the required time and sprinkle with half the parsley and garlic. Cook the other side until done to your liking, and turn again. Sprinkle the remaining garlic, parsley and chives (if using) over the top and add the Worcestershire sauce. Heat the brandy in a separate pan, set it alight if you like (not essential) and pour over the steak. Shake the pan to distribute the sauce, turn the steak over in it, then transfer to a warmed hot plate and pour the pan juices over.
Serves 1

◆ *Tournedos à la Rossini* ◆

FATIMA WHITBREAD, ATHLETE

Grill the steaks rather than frying them if you prefer. If you cannot get (or afford) truffles, use cooked mushrooms instead.

4 fillet steaks
4 slices of bread, crusts removed
3oz (75g) butter or 2oz (50g)
   butter and 1 tablespoon
   vegetable oil

For the sauce:
4 tablespoons brown stock
4 tablespoons Madeira
For the garnish:
4 slices pâté
4 truffles
Watercress

Tie the steaks into rounds, or ask the butcher to do this for you.

Fry the slices of bread (cut into rounds if you wish) in hot butter (or butter and oil) in a large frying pan until crisp and golden brown. Transfer to a hot serving dish and keep warm.

Fry the steaks on both sides. If you like your steak rare, cook over a high heat very briefly and serve almost at once; for medium-done steak, cook each side for 2 to 3 minutes at a high temperature, then lower the heat and cook for a further 2 to 3 minutes; for well-done steak, cook each side for 2 to 3 minutes on high, then allow a further 4 to 5 minutes. Lift each steak on to a slice of fried bread and keep warm.

Blend the stock and Madeira together in the frying pan, heat until simmering, stirring constantly, and pour around the steaks. Top each steak with a slice of pâté and a truffle. Garnish with watercress and serve at once with sauté potatoes.
Serves 4

◆ *Beef Satay* ◆
RUTH MADOC OF *HI-DE-HI!*

1 tablespoon blanched almonds
1 tablespoon root ginger, peeled and sliced
1 teaspoon ground coriander
1 teaspoon turmeric
10fl oz (300ml) coconut milk

1½lb (750g) lean beef (sirloin or rump), cut into bite-sized pieces
Salt and black pepper
1 teaspoon brown sugar (or to taste)

Pound the almonds, ginger, coriander and turmeric to a paste in a mortar and gradually dilute with coconut milk. Sprinkle the meat with salt and pepper and marinate in the spiced coconut milk for 2 hours.

Remove the meat from the marinade and thread on to skewers. Sprinkle with a little sugar and grill, turning and basting frequently with the marinade.

Serve with satay sauce, allowing two skewers per person.
Serves 4

◆ *Satay Sauce* ◆
RUTH MADOC OF *HI-DE-HI!*

2 onions
1–2 tablespoons peanut oil
3oz (75g) roasted peanuts
½ teaspoon chilli powder

1 teaspoon light brown sugar
Salt
1 tablespoon soya sauce
Juice of ½ lime

Thinly slice 1 onion and fry in the hot peanut oil until transparent. Finely chop the second onion and pound it to a paste with the peanuts and chilli powder in a mortar. Add this paste to the frying onion and fry for a further 3 minutes, stirring continuously. Gradually dilute the mixture with 5fl oz (150ml) warm water and stir in the sugar. Cook for a few minutes until the sauce has the consistency of single cream. Season to taste with salt, soya sauce and lime juice. Serve hot.

◆ Beef Wellington ◆

RT HON NORMAN TEBBIT, MP,
CHAIRMAN OF THE CONSERVATIVE PARTY

2lb (1kg) fillet of beef
Pepper
1oz (25g) butter
4oz (125g) button mushrooms,
  sliced
1 dessertspoon chopped mixed
  herbs, including parsley

8oz (250g) puff pastry, thawed if
  frozen
8oz (250g) smooth pâté
Beaten egg to glaze
Watercress to garnish

Pre-heat the oven to gas mark 7, 425°F (220°C).

Trim and tie up the fillet. Pepper it and brown it quickly all over in hot butter, then roast in the oven for 10 minutes. Remove from the oven and allow to cool.

In the meantime, sauté the mushrooms in butter for a few minutes, remove from the heat, add the herbs and cool.

Roll out the pastry into a rectangle, cutting off a thin strip from which to make the decorations. Divide it into two pieces, one two-thirds larger than the other. Put the mushroom mixture on the larger piece. Slice the meat in half lengthways and spread pâté on it, then lay it on the mushroom mixture. Press the edges of the pastry up around it. Lay the other piece of pastry over the top and secure well. Brush with beaten egg to glaze, and decorate with fleurons (small crescent-shaped pieces of pastry made from the trimmings). Bake in the oven at gas mark 7, 425°F (220°C) for 10 minutes, then reduce the heat to gas mark 4, 350°F (180°C) for a further 30 minutes or until the pastry is well browned and cooked through. Serve hot or cold, garnished with watercress.
Serves 4

◆ *Hungarian Goulash* ◆

LADY HOWE, WIFE OF SIR GEOFFREY HOWE, MP,
FOREIGN SECRETARY

1 tablespoon olive oil
1½lb (750g) stewing steak, cut
  into small cubes
2 large onions, roughly chopped
1 clove of garlic, crushed
1 rounded tablespoon plain flour
1 rounded tablespoon Hungarian
  paprika

1 × 14oz (400g) tin tomatoes
Salt and pepper
1 medium green pepper, cored,
  de-seeded and cut into strips
5fl oz (150ml) soured cream

Pre-heat the oven to gas mark 3, 325°F (170°C).

Heat the oil in a flameproof casserole until sizzling. Add the cubes of beef and fry until brown. Transfer to a plate.

Turn the heat down a little and fry the onions until pale golden. Add the garlic and return the meat to the casserole. Sprinkle in the flour and paprika. Add the tomatoes and season with salt and pepper. Bring to the boil, cover with a tight-fitting lid and cook on the middle shelf of the oven for 2 hours. Add the green pepper to the casserole and cook for a further 30 minutes.

Just before serving, stir in the soured cream and sprinkle a little more paprika over the dish. This can be served with rice and perhaps a green salad.
Serves 4

◆ *Steak and Kidney Pie* ◆

RT HON MICHAEL R. D. HESELTINE, MP

Vegetable oil or dripping
1½lb (750g) stewing steak, cubed
8oz (250g) lamb's kidneys, cored
   and roughly chopped
1 medium onion, sliced
2 heaped tablespoons flour
2 tablespoons tomato purée
1–1½ pints (600–850ml) stock

5fl oz (150ml) red wine
4oz (125g) mushrooms, sliced
Salt and pepper
Chopped parsley and basil
12oz (350g) puff pastry, thawed if
   frozen
Beaten egg to glaze

Pre-heat the oven to gas mark 6, 400°F (200°C).

Heat the oil or dripping in a flameproof casserole, add the steak, kidneys and onion and fry until the meat is lightly browned. Sprinkle the flour over and put the casserole, uncovered, into the oven for 5 minutes to allow the flour to soak up the fat. Then remove from the oven, add the tomato purée and mix well. Add the stock, wine, mushrooms, salt, pepper, chopped parsley and a large pinch of basil. Bring to the boil and simmer for 1 hour. Adjust the seasoning and transfer to a pie dish.

Roll out the pastry so that it is slightly larger than the top of the pie dish. Put a strip of pastry round the edge of the dish, brush with water and cover the dish with the pastry lid. Cut the sides of the pastry with a knife and decorate the top with leaves made from the pastry trimmings. Brush with beaten egg and bake in the oven at gas mark 6, 400°F (200°C) for 10 minutes. Reduce the temperature to gas mark 4, 350°F (180°C) and bake for a further 20 to 25 minutes.

Serves 4

◆ *Country Pie* ◆

LORD (TED) WILLIS, PLAYWRIGHT AND AUTHOR

1lb (500g) good-quality minced beef
Vegetable oil
Brown gravy

3 tablespoons sage and onion stuffing mix
2lb (1kg) mashed potatoes

Pre-heat the oven to gas mark 4, 350°F (180°C).

Fry the minced beef in the oil until brown, then strain off the fat. Add the gravy and stuffing mix and continue cooking until fairly thick, stirring all the time.

Grease a large pie dish and line with some of the mashed potato. Add the meat mixture and top with the rest of the potato. Fork over the top. Bake in the oven for 1 hour. Serve with fried onions and peas.
Serves 4

◆ *Koftes (Greek Meat Balls)* ◆

COSTAS ONISIFOROU, BAKER AND FRIEND OF FARRINGTONS SCHOOL

1lb (500g) minced beef
1 large potato, grated
1 medium onion, grated
4oz (125g) breadcrumbs
4 tablespoons finely chopped parsley

1 tablespoon finely chopped mint
½ teaspoon cinnamon
1 egg, beaten
Salt and pepper
Olive oil for frying

Mix all the ingredients together, divide into small balls and roll them between the palms of the hands. Fry in a little olive oil, and serve hot or cold with a salad.

◆ *Dry Curry* ◆

LORD HAILSHAM, FORMER LORD CHANCELLOR

You can use any cooked meat, well minced, instead of fresh beef mince for this recipe, but of course the cooking time will then be much shorter. Remember that curry is a way of eating rice, so serve with plenty of rice. I serve poppadoms too. I drink beer with curry: do not waste wine on it. Water or cider are also both acceptable.

1 large onion chopped
Vegetable oil
1lb (500g) minced beef
1 apple, peeled, cored and sliced
    into rounds
1 tomato, peeled, de-seeded and
    chopped (see page 91) or 1
    tablespoon tomato purée or
    ketchup

1 banana, sliced
Left-over cooked vegetables,
    chopped
1oz (25g) sultanas
Curry powder
Cider or water
Salt

Sauté the onion in the oil until transparent. Add the minced beef, apple, tomato or tomato purée or ketchup, banana, cooked vegetables and sultanas. Fry for a few minutes, stirring occasionally until the meat has browned a little. Add curry powder to taste and fry, stirring, for a further minute. Add as little cider or water as you can get away with, and salt to taste. Bring to the boil, cover and simmer gently for about 1 hour.

◆ *Shepherd's Pie* ◆

BETTY KING, EX-FARRINGTONS SCHOOL POSTWOMAN

1 large onion, sliced
Vegetable oil
1lb (500g) minced beef
1 tablespoon tomato ketchup
1 tablespoon HP sauce
1 tablespoon gravy powder

2 tablespoons baked beans or
  grated carrots
2lb (1kg) potatoes, cut into
  chunks
Salt and pepper
Butter
1 tomato, sliced

Fry the onion in a little oil until soft. Add the minced beef and fry until lightly browned. Transfer to an ovenproof dish. In a bowl combine 5fl oz (150ml) water, the sauces and gravy powder and pour over the minced beef. Top with the baked beans or carrots.

   Cook the potatoes in simmering salted water until tender, drain, add a knob of butter and pepper to taste and mash until smooth. Spread over the mixture in the ovenproof dish and arrange the tomato slices on top. Bake in the oven at gas mark 4, 350°F (180°C) for 30 minutes until the potato is lightly browned.
Serves 4

◆ *Stuffed Marrow* ◆

JUNE WHITFIELD, COMEDIENNE

Cook your favourite mince recipe to make the stuffing for the marrow.

1lb minced beef or lamb, stewed   Butter
1 medium marrow   Cheddar cheese, grated
Salt

Pre-heat the oven to gas mark 4, 350°F (180°C).

Peel and de-seed the marrow and cut in half lengthways. Cook in very little boiling salted water with a knob of butter for 10 to 15 minutes until tender but not mushy. Drain.

Place the marrow halves side by side in a large greased ovenproof dish. Fill the hollows with the stewed minced beef or lamb and scatter some cheese on top. Cover and bake in the oven for 1 hour.

Before serving, sprinkle with more cheese and put under the grill for a few minutes to brown. Serve with mashed potatoes.

◆*Veal Escalope with Cream and Mushrooms* ◆

KARL WINKLER, EXECUTIVE HEAD CHEF ABOARD THE LINER
QUEEN ELIZABETH II AND FARRINGTONS SCHOOL PARENT

4 veal escalopes
1oz (25g) butter
3 small shallots, finely chopped
8oz (250g) mushrooms, sliced
1 glass white wine

5fl oz (150ml) double cream
Lemon juice
2 tablespoons Madeira
Chopped parsley

Sauté the veal in the butter until just cooked. Remove and keep warm.
Sauté the shallots and mushrooms lightly in the remaining butter, add
the white wine and reduce. Stir in the cream and reduce further until
lightly thickened. Add a little lemon juice and *beurre manié*. Finish the
sauce with the Madeira. Coat the veal escalope with the sauce and serve
sprinkled with chopped parsley. Turned mushrooms may be added for
the final presentation.
Serves 4

◆ *West Country Summer Pork* ◆

RT HON TOM KING, MP, SECRETARY OF STATE FOR NORTHERN IRELAND

2½lb (1.25kg) pork, boned and
   cubed
Seasoned flour
2 tablespoons vegetable oil
1 clove of garlic (optional)
8oz (250g) onions, finely chopped
8oz (250g) carrots, sliced
1 stock cube – pork, chicken or
   lamb flavour

1 bouquet garni
Black pepper
Salt (optional)
8oz (250g) green beans
1 tablespoon lemon juice
1lb (500g) small new potatoes
10fl oz (300ml) Taunton or
   scrumpy cider

Pre-heat the oven to gas mark 3, 325°F (170°C).

Dust the pork with seasoned flour. Heat the oil in a large frying pan, add the pork and fry to seal. Transfer to a large ovenproof casserole.

Lightly fry the garlic, onions and carrots in the remaining oil. Sprinkle with 1 tablespoon seasoned flour to soak up the juices, and add to the pork. Then add all the other ingredients except the cider and mix well. Gently pour in the cider and cover the casserole. Cook in the oven for 2 to 2½ hours. Serve with broccoli.

Serves 6

◆ *Fried Pork with Bean Sprouts* ◆

ROSALIND PATEY, FRIEND OF FARRINGTONS SCHOOL

You can substitute chicken or prawns for the pork in this recipe, but if you do, *do not* use bicarbonate of soda. When buying bean sprouts, look for short fat ones and make sure that the root is not black. If you don't like garlic, use a finely chopped pickled onion instead. The light-coloured sesame oil sold in health food shops in Britain is not the correct one for Chinese cooking; it lacks flavour. You need the slightly brown-coloured one with a stronger smell.

8oz (250g) pork escalopes, cut
   into thin strips
¼ teaspoon salt
10oz (300g) bean sprouts or 1
   green and 1 red pepper, cored,
   de-seeded and cut into thin
   strips
Vegetable oil for frying
3 cloves of garlic, crushed
6 large button mushrooms, sliced
4 spring onions, chopped

For the seasoning:
½ teaspoon bicarbonate of soda
¼ teaspoon sugar
1 teaspoon light soya sauce
¼ teaspoon pepper
2 teaspoons oyster sauce
1 teaspoon sesame oil
1 teaspoon cornflour
1 tablespoon corn oil
1 teaspoon dry sherry or rice wine

In a bowl combine the bicarbonate, sugar, light soya sauce, pepper and oyster sauce. Add the pork and mix well. Mix the sesame oil, cornflour, corn oil and sherry or rice wine together. Add this to the pork and leave to marinate for at least 30 minutes (or overnight if you prefer).

Add the salt to the bean sprouts (if using) and mix well. Heat 2 tablespoons oil in a wok or heavy frying pan and stir-fry the bean sprouts for about 2 minutes (do not overcook or they will be soggy). Remove the bean sprouts from the wok and set aside.

Add another teaspoon of oil to the wok and heat until very hot (most important when cooking pork). Add the garlic, the pork and its marinade and the peppers (if using instead of bean sprouts). Stir-fry for a few minutes then add the mushrooms and any juice from the bean sprouts; fry for a few more minutes, stirring constantly. Return the bean sprouts to the wok, add the spring onions and stir-fry for a further minute. Serve immediately.

Serves 2

◆ *Chilli con Carne* ◆

STEVE CRAM, ATHLETE

2 medium onions, sliced
1 clove of garlic, crushed
1 tablespoon olive oil
1lb (500g) minced beef
1 × 15oz (425g) tin red kidney
   beans, drained
5fl oz (150ml) beef stock
1 bay leaf

2 tablespoons tomato purée
1 × 14oz (400g) tin tomatoes
1 × 15oz (425g) tin baked beans
1 teaspoon dried mixed herbs
Salt and freshly ground pepper
1½ teaspoons hot chilli powder
Dash of Worcestershire sauce

Fry the onions and garlic in the olive oil in a large pan until soft. Add the minced beef and fry until well browned. Add the kidney beans, beef stock and bay leaf. Stir and add the tomato purée and tomatoes. Stir and add the baked beans and mixed herbs. Season with salt, pepper, chilli powder and Worcestershire sauce. Bring to the boil and simmer for at least 1 hour.

Serve on jacket potatoes or rice, or with garlic bread.

Serves 4 to 6

◆ *Lamb's Kidneys Cooked in Butter and Mustard Sauce* ◆

RT HON DR DAVID OWEN, MP,
LEADER OF THE SOCIAL DEMOCRATIC PARTY

Butter
6 lamb's kidneys, outer skin and
    fat removed
1 tablespoon spring onion or
    ordinary onion, finely chopped

3 fl oz (75ml) dry white wine
1 tablespoon Dijon mustard
Salt and pepper
Chopped parsley

Melt a knob of butter in a shallow flameproof casserole or deep frying pan. Add the kidneys and fry gently for about 10 minutes, turning half-way through, by which time they should be cooked on the outside and pink in the centre. Transfer to a warmed plate and keep warm.

Add the onion to the butter in the casserole and fry for 1 minute. Then add the white wine and bring to the boil while scraping up the bits on the bottom of the casserole. Take off the heat, and add the mustard and a further 1 tablespoon butter along with salt and pepper to taste. Slice the kidneys about ¼ in. (6mm) thick at a slight angle, then return to the casserole. Set over a low heat for a couple of minutes to heat the kidneys through. Add a sprinkling of parsley and serve with boiled rice.
Serves 2

◆ *Liver Stir-fry* ◆

DAVID JASON, ACTOR

3 tablespoons vegetable oil
1 small cauliflower, divided into
    small florets
1 red onion, chopped
3 rashers bacon, de-rinded and
    chopped
8oz (250g) lamb's liver, cut into
    strips

4oz (125g) mushrooms, sliced
8oz (250g) white cabbage,
    shredded
8oz (250g) peas
1 dessertspoon soya sauce
Large pinch of dried mixed herbs
Freshly ground pepper
4fl oz (125ml) stock or water

Ensure that all the vegetables are cut into pieces of roughly equal size
before you start to cook.

Heat the oil in a large heavy frying pan till very hot and fry the
cauliflower, onion and bacon for 3 minutes, stirring all the time. Then
add the liver, mushrooms, cabbage, peas, soya sauce, herbs and pepper,
continuing to stir. Cook for 3 minutes more, then add the stock or water
and cook for 3 minutes on a low heat. Serve with boiled rice or mashed
potatoes.
Serves 4 to 6

◆ *Ox Liver Casserole* ◆

SUE LAWLEY, TELEVISION JOURNALIST

1lb (500g) ox liver
1oz (25g) plain flour
Salt and pepper
1oz (25g) dripping
2 large onions, roughly chopped

2 medium leeks, cut into 1in.
   (2.5cm) slices
3 large carrots, thinly sliced
5fl oz (150ml) beer (optional)
1 teaspoon dried mixed herbs

Pre-heat the oven to gas mark 3, 325°F (170°C).

Rinse the liver, removing any skin or tubes, and cut it into even-sized chunks. Mix the flour with a good pinch of both salt and pepper and toss the liver in this, coating it on all sides.

Melt the dripping in a frying pan and fry the vegetables for 5 minutes, then transfer them to a casserole, leaving as much fat in the pan as possible. Fry the liver in the remaining fat until it is brown on all sides. Mix with the vegetables in the casserole.

Pour the beer (or water if you prefer) into the frying pan and bring to the boil, stirring all the time. Add the herbs and more salt and pepper to taste, and pour over the liver. Cover the casserole with a lid and cook in the oven for about 1 hour or until the liver is tender. Serve with 3oz (75g) mashed potatoes per person.

Serves 4

◆*Westphalian Salad* ◆

WEST GERMAN EMBASSY

11oz (325g) boiled potatoes,
 diced
1 large eating apple, cored and
 diced
2 celery sticks, thinly sliced
2oz (50g) shelled walnuts,
 coarsely chopped

3 tablespoons German
 mayonnaise
Apple slices to garnish
1 teaspoon lemon juice
8 slices Westphalian ham

Put the potatoes, diced apple, celery, walnuts and mayonnaise in a bowl and mix well. Garnish with slices of apple dipped in lemon juice to prevent them turning brown. Serve with the Westphalian ham.

As an alternative, wrap slices of Westphalian ham around canned asparagus tips, and serve with hollandaise sauce.
Serves 4

•Poultry & Game•

◆ *Chicken with Mint and Yogurt* ◆

BERYL REID, ACTRESS AND COMEDIENNE

Juice of 1 lemon
2–3 tablespoons sunflower or
   olive oil
1 large clove of garlic, crushed
1 teaspoon turmeric
2–3 teaspoons powdered cumin

1 large handful chopped fresh
   mint or 1 tablespoon dried
   mint
Salt and pepper
6 chicken joints, skinned
5 fl oz (150ml) natural yogurt

Mix together the lemon juice, oil, garlic, spices, mint, salt and pepper in a glass or earthenware bowl. Lay the chicken joints in the mixture and brush it over them so that they are well coated. Leave to marinate for at least 1 hour.

Heat the oven to gas mark 4, 350°F (180°C). Transfer the chicken and marinade to a lidded ovenproof casserole and bake in the oven for 1½ hours. Before serving, stir the yogurt into the cooking juices and warm through. Serve the chicken with new potatoes or rice, with the yogurt sauce spooned over.
Serves 6

◆ *Indian Spatchcock Chicken* ◆

LADY RING, WIFE OF SIR LINDSAY RING,
FORMER LORD MAYOR OF LONDON

2oz (50g) butter
4–6 chicken portions, skinned
1 large onion, sliced
15fl oz (450ml) chicken stock

For the sauce:
1½ teaspoons dry mustard
1½ teaspoons anchovy essence
3 dessertspoons brown sugar
6 tablespoons mushroom ketchup
6 tablespoons stock
Cayenne pepper
5fl oz (150ml) double cream

Melt the butter in a large pan and fry the chicken portions and onion in it until the chicken is lightly browned and the onion softened. Add the stock, stir well, put the lid on and simmer gently for 40 minutes or until the chicken is tender.

Meanwhile prepare the sauce. Place all the ingredients except the cream in a pan and heat, stirring, to boiling point. Simmer for 2 minutes. Remove from the heat and add the cream – warm through gently but *do not boil.*

Remove the cooked chicken from the stock and place in a serving dish. Serve with the sauce poured over.
Serves 4 to 6

◆ *Poulet Basquaise* ◆

FRANCINE HAAS, FARRINGTONS SCHOOL HOUSEMISTRESS

3lb (1.5kg) chicken, cut into 6
   portions
Olive oil
Salt and pepper
4fl oz (125ml) dry white wine

Pinch of mixed herbs
2 large red peppers
2 large green peppers
4 medium tomatoes
6 medium onions, finely chopped

Fry the chicken pieces in olive oil until lightly browned. Transfer to a flameproof casserole, add salt and pepper to taste, the white wine and the mixed herbs. Bring to the boil, then leave to simmer gently.

Meanwhile grill the whole peppers under a hot grill, turning regularly, until the skin is blistered all over. Wrap each pepper in a piece of wet kitchen paper and set aside.

Put the tomatoes in a heatproof bowl, pour boiling water over them, leave for a few seconds, then plunge into cold water. Remove the skins, which will now slide off easily, and chop the flesh, discarding the seeds.

Unwrap the peppers and remove the skins, which will now peel off easily. Chop the flesh, discarding the stalk, core and seeds.

Fry the chopped peppers with the onions in olive oil for about 10 minutes, until the onions are soft but not brown, then add the chopped tomatoes. Continue to cook gently until a creamy mixture results. Add this to the simmering chicken. Taste and adjust the seasoning, and continue to simmer over a gentle heat for about 20 minutes or until the chicken is cooked through and tender.
Serves 6

◆ *Chicken Sauté Majorca* ◆

ELIZABETH WALLACE, FARRINGTONS SCHOOL
EX-GOVERNOR

1 tablespoon olive oil
¾oz (20g) butter
2½lb (1.25kg) chicken, cut into 6
   portions
1 large onion, thinly sliced
1 level dessertspoon flour
1 glass white wine or dry cider
5fl oz (150ml) giblet stock

Salt and pepper
1 bouquet garni
1 bayleaf
1 large orange
1 red pepper, de-seeded and very
   thinly sliced
12 small green olives, stoned
1 tablespoon chopped parsley

Heat the oil and butter in a large frying pan. When foaming, put in the chicken joints, skin side down, and sauté until golden brown, turning so that they are cooked on all sides. Remove from the pan and keep warm.

Now add the onion to the pan and sauté until barely coloured. Stir in the flour, add the wine and stock, and bring to the boil. Season to taste with salt and pepper and replace the chicken joints. Add the bouquet garni and bayleaf, cover the pan and simmer for 20 to 25 minutes or until the chicken is cooked through and tender. Meanwhile, cut the rind and pith from the orange, reserving a strip of peel. Slice the flesh thinly into rounds.

Remove the cooked chicken joints from their cooking sauce, trim them, arrange on a hot serving dish and keep warm. Add the red pepper, orange slices and strip of peel, olives and parsley to the sauce and simmer for about 5 minutes. Remove the bouquet garni, bayleaf and orange peel and spoon the sauce over the chicken joints to serve.
Serves 6

◆ *Tandoori-style Chicken* ◆

SHEZAD HUSAIN, COOKERY WRITER AND FARRINGTONS
SCHOOL PARENT

The following recipe is reproduced from my book *Entertaining Indian Style*.

4 chicken quarters, skinned
5fl oz (150ml) natural yogurt
1½ teaspoons root ginger,
 crushed
1½ teaspoons garlic, crushed
1 teaspoon chilli powder
2 teaspoons ground cumin

1 teaspoon salt
2 teaspoons ground coriander
½ teaspoon red food colouring
1 tablespoon tamarind paste
5fl oz (150ml) water
5fl oz (150ml) vegetable oil

Marinate the chicken in the yogurt, with the ginger, garlic, spices, salt
and colouring well blended in a large bowl, for a minimum of 3 hours.

In a separate bowl mix the tamarind paste with the water, using a fork,
and fold into the yogurt marinade. Rub this over the chicken pieces and
set aside for a further 3 hours.

Place the chicken pieces in a heatproof dish. Brush the top with oil.
Pre-heat the grill, turn the heat down to medium and place the chicken
under the grill, not too close to the heat. Grill for 30 to 35 minutes,
turning twice and basting with the remaining oil.

Arrange the cooked chicken on a bed of lettuce and garnish with onion
rings, sliced tomatoes and lemon wedges.
Serves 4

◆ *Brandy Chicken with Apricots* ◆

RICHARD O'SULLIVAN, ACTOR

2oz (50g) dried apricots
2 chicken breasts
Salt and pepper
Flour
Butter

Vegetable oil
Brandy
Natural yogurt
Lemon juice

Simmer the apricots in water for about 10 minutes. Flatten the two chicken breasts between sheets of greaseproof paper into an escalope shape. Coat with seasoned flour and fry in the butter and oil until browned and almost cooked through. Set aside and keep warm.

Flambée the apricots in the brandy. Mix in the yogurt and lemon juice and season to taste with salt and pepper. Put the chicken pieces in a large pan, pour the apricot mixture over and simmer gently for 5 to 10 minutes. Serve with rice or noodles.

Serves 2

◆ *Chicken and Leek Pie* ◆

MICHAEL CRAWFORD, COMEDIAN, ACTOR AND SINGER

1 chicken, jointed
Stock or water
1lb (500g) leeks
Salt and pepper

5fl oz (150ml) cream (optional)
8oz (250g) flaky pastry, thawed if
    frozen
Beaten egg to glaze

Simmer the chicken joints gently in the stock or water for 30 minutes. Cut the leeks in half lengthways and then cut into 2in. (5cm) pieces. Tie together, add to the chicken and cook for a further 15 minutes. Strain, reserving the stock.

Heat the oven to gas mark 8, 450°F (230°C).

Remove the chicken flesh from the bones and put it with the leeks in a pie dish. Season well with salt and pepper. Add the cream (if using) and enough of the reserved stock to moisten. Roll out the pastry to fit the pie dish and use to cover the chicken and leek filling. Decorate the top of the pie and glaze with a little beaten egg. Bake in the oven for 10 minutes, then reduce the heat to gas mark 5, 375°F (190°C) and bake for a further 25 minutes or until the pastry is golden brown and cooked through.
Serves 4 to 6

◆ *Chicken Espagnole* ◆

LADY DAVIS, FORMER LADY MAYORESS OF LONDON

2oz (50g) butter
4 chicken joints
1 rasher of bacon, cut into small
   pieces
1 medium onion, chopped
2oz (50g) flour
1 pint (600ml) chicken stock
1 carrot, thinly sliced

1 × 5oz (150g) tin tomato purée
1 bay leaf
1 bouquet garni
1 tablespoon dried red or green
   peppers
4oz (125g) mushrooms, sliced
Salt and pepper
3 tablespoons sherry

Pre-heat the oven to gas mark 3, 325°F (170°C).

Heat the butter in a large pan and fry the chicken joints until golden. Remove and set aside to keep warm. Fry the bacon and onion lightly. Stir in the flour and gradually add the stock. Bring to the boil, stirring all the time. Add the carrot, tomato purée, bay leaf, bouquet garni, peppers and mushrooms. Season to taste with salt and pepper. Put the chicken in an ovenproof casserole and pour over the sauce. Bake in the oven for about 1 hour or until the chicken is tender. Stir in the sherry 15 minutes before the end end of the cooking time. Remove the bay leaf and bouquet garni before serving.
Serves 4

◆ *Poulet Gratiné au Porto* ◆

DENISE ROBERTSON, EX-FARRINGTONS SCHOOL FRENCH
CONVERSATION TEACHER

6 chicken portions (preferably
  boneless)
1½oz (40g) butter
1 tablespoon flour
1 small glass of port
2 shallots, chopped

1 bouquet garni or 1 tablespoon
  mixed herbs
Salt and pepper
5fl oz (150ml) double cream
2oz (50g) Gruyère cheese, grated

Fry the chicken portions in the butter until golden, then sprinkle with the flour and cook for a further 1 minute, stirring. Add the port and bring to the boil, continuing to stir. If the resulting sauce is too thick, add more port mixed with water until you get a fairly liquid sauce. Add the shallots, bouquet garni or mixed herbs and salt and pepper to taste. Partly cover the pan and simmer for 30 minutes over a very low heat (the sauce must barely boil) until the chicken is cooked through and tender.

Transfer the chicken to an ovenproof dish suitable for serving. Strain the sauce, add the cream and pour it over the chicken pieces. Sprinkle with the grated cheese and bake in the oven at gas mark 5, 375°F (190°C) until the cheese is golden brown.

Serves 6

◆ *Supreme of Chicken with King Crabmeat* ◆

KARL WINKLER, EXECUTIVE HEAD CHEF ABOARD THE LINER
QUEEN ELIZABETH II AND FARRINGTONS SCHOOL PARENT

1 chicken breast
2 spinach leaves, shredded
1 stick of king crab, chopped
Chicken stock
2 tomatoes, *concassés* (skinned,
   de-seeded and chopped – see
   page 91)

1 pint (600ml) cream
1 cup chicken *velouté*
Unsalted butter
Parsley sprigs to garnish

Prepare the chicken breast and stuff with the spinach leaves mixed with
the crabmeat. Roll in aluminium foil and poach in chicken stock until
just cooked through. Remove from the stock and keep warm. Reduce
the stock, add the tomatoes and cream and reduce further. Liquidize the
sauce in a blender until smooth, then finish with a little *velouté* and
unsalted butter. Slice the chicken neatly. Coat a plate with the sauce and
arrange the chicken slices on it. Serve garnished with parsley.
Serves 1

◆ *Chicken in Creamy Orange Sauce* ◆

VALERIE SINGLETON, TELEVISION PRESENTER

4 portions cooked chicken

For the sauce:
1 tin concentrated orange juice
1 pint (600ml) cream

2 tablespoons finely grated root
   ginger
3–4 cloves of garlic, crushed
3 tablespoons soya sauce

Mix all the ingredients together and pour over the chicken. Serve with
salad.
Serves 4

◆ *Chicken Casserole* ◆

JULIA McKENZIE, SINGER AND ACTRESS

Corn-fed chicken is especially delicious in this dish which may be made in advance and stored overnight in the refrigerator for re-heating the following day.

1 large onion, chopped
Vegetable oil
2½lb (1.25kg) chicken, jointed
8oz (250g) dried prunes
8oz (250g) dried apricots

Chicken stock
White wine
Brown sugar
Salt and pepper

Pre-heat the oven to gas mark 4, 350°F (180°C).

In a heavy flameproof casserole, fry the onion in the oil. Remove, then fry the chicken portions until golden. Return the onion to the casserole and add the prunes and apricots. Barely cover with stock and wine, and add a little brown sugar, salt and pepper to taste. Cover the casserole, place in the oven and cook for 1½ to 2 hours. The finished dish should have a sticky consistency.
Serves 4 to 6

◆ *Chicken in Barbecue Sauce* ◆

SARAH LOVETT-SMITH, FARRINGTONS SCHOOL PUPIL

4 chicken portions
For the sauce:
16fl oz (475ml) tomato sauce
1 large onion, chopped
1 clove of garlic, minced

5fl oz (150ml) soya sauce
2 tablespoons brown sugar
1 teaspoon dry mustard
¼ teaspoon cayenne pepper

Pre-heat the oven to gas mark 5, 375°F (190°C).

Mix all the sauce ingredients together and pour over the chicken pieces in a well-greased ovenproof dish. Cook uncovered in the oven for about 1 hour or until the chicken is tender.
Serves 4

◆ *Breast of Duckling with Mixed Berries* ◆

KARL WINKLER, EXECUTIVE HEAD CHEF ABOARD THE LINER QUEEN ELIZABETH II AND FARRINGTONS SCHOOL PARENT

2 duckling breasts, skinned
Salt and pepper
Unsalted butter
Wine vinegar
Brown sugar

Veal gravy
Raspberries
Blackberries
Crème de cassis

Season the duckling breasts with salt and pepper and sauté in butter in a pan, leaving them slightly underdone. Remove from the pan and keep warm. Rinse the pan with wine vinegar and brown sugar, and add a little veal gravy and some of the berries. Simmer for a few minutes, then liquidize and strain. Finish the sauce with crème de cassis and butter. Carve the duckling breasts very thinly and arrange neatly on a serving plate coated with the sauce. Garnish with heaps of raspberries and blackberries that have been glazed in butter and sugar.
Serves 2

◆ *Chicken Salad* ◆

LISA HARTMAN OF *KNOTS LANDING*

You can add any other raw fresh vegetables of your choice – such as thinly sliced onions or courgettes – to make this delicious salad. For those who are counting calories I recommend a low-calorie Italian dressing.

Cooked chicken, skinned and
  diced
Lettuce, shredded
Sprouts, chopped if large
Tomatoes, chopped

Avocado pear, peeled, stoned
  and diced
Mushrooms, thinly sliced
Dressing

Combine all the ingredients in a large bowl. Add a dressing of your choice and mix well.

♦Puddings
ℰ Sweets♦

◆ *Pumpkin Pecan Pie* ◆

NANCY REAGAN, FIRST LADY OF THE USA

1 × 9in. (23cm) shortcrust pastry case

For the filling:
4 eggs, lightly beaten
2 cups canned or mashed cooked pumpkin

1 cup sugar
½ cup dark corn syrup
1 teaspoon vanilla essence
½ teaspoon cinnamon
¼ teaspoon salt
1 cup pecan nuts, chopped

Pre-heat the oven to gas mark 4, 350°F (180°C).
   Combine all the filling ingredients except the pecans. Pour into the pastry case and top with the pecans. Bake in the oven for 40 minutes, or until set.
Serves 6

◆ *Lemon Crunch* ◆

PAUL DANIELS, MAGICIAN

4oz (125g) ginger nut biscuits, crushed
2oz (50g) butter, melted
4fl oz (125ml) double cream

1 × 7oz (200g) tin condensed milk
2 lemons
Grated chocolate to garnish

Mix the biscuit crumbs with the melted butter. Use to line a 9in. (23cm) flan dish and chill in the refrigerator. Lightly whip the cream and mix with the condensed milk. Add the grated rind of 1 lemon and the juice of both until you can no longer taste the condensed milk. When well mixed and really thick, pour into the lined flan dish and return to the refrigerator. Remove 1 hour before serving and decorate with grated chocolate.
Serves 4 to 6

◆ *Blushing Bride* ◆

LADY RING, WIFE OF SIR LINDSAY RING, FORMER LORD MAYOR OF LONDON

Castor sugar
1lb (500g) raspberries (fresh or
  frozen)
10fl oz (300ml) double cream
1 egg white

8oz (250g) rough-textured
  continental rye bread (not
  pumpernickel), crumbled

Sprinkle sugar on the raspberries to sweeten. Whip the cream until it stands in soft peaks; beat the egg white until stiff but not dry. Fold 1 dessertspoon sugar into the cream, followed the the beaten egg white. Put half the crumbled rye bread in a glass bowl, dust lightly with sugar, then add half the sweetened raspberries, then half the cream. Repeat in the same order. This sweet is best made several hours in advance and left in the refrigerator to chill.

◆ *Banana and Toffee Pie* ◆

RT HON MARGARET THATCHER, MP,
LEADER OF THE CONSERVATIVE PARTY AND PRIME
MINISTER, EX-FARRINGTONS SCHOOL PARENT

8oz (250g) shortcrust pastry
1 × 14oz (400g) tin condensed
  milk
3–4 large bananas

10fl oz (300ml) double cream
2 level teaspoons instant coffee

Pre-heat the oven to gas mark 5, 375°F (190°C).

Roll out the pastry and use to line a 9in. (23cm) flan dish. Bake blind in the oven for about 20 minutes. Allow to cool.

Place the unopened tin of condensed milk in a large lidded saucepan and cover with cold water. Bring slowly to the boil and simmer for 2 hours, keeping the tin well submerged in water the whole time. Allow the tin to cool.

Open the cooled tin: the condensed milk should now be pale brown and of a toffee-like consistency. Spread the toffee mixture on to the pastry, and slice the bananas on to the toffee layer. Whip the cream until it stands in soft peaks, add the coffee and mix well. Spread the cream over the banana layer and serve.

Serves 6

◆ *Pavlova* ◆

BONNIE LANGFORD, ACTRESS, SINGER AND DANCER

3 egg whites
6oz (175g) castor sugar
1 teaspoon vanilla essence
1 teaspoon vinegar
1 teaspoon cornflour

10fl oz (300ml) double cream
Raspberries, strawberries,
pineapple, apricots, or other
fruit of your choice, tinned
(and drained) or fresh

Pre-heat the oven to gas mark 1, 275°F (140°C).

Beat the egg whites until very stiff. Add the sugar gradually, continuing to beat until it has dissolved. Fold in the vanilla, vinegar and cornflour. Spread the mixture on a greased 8in. (20cm) round of greaseproof paper placed on a baking tray, making the sides higher than the centre to form a shell. Bake in the oven for 1 hour. When the meringue shell is cool, carefully remove the greaseproof paper and place on a flat tray or board. Whip the cream until it stands in soft peaks and use to fill the meringue shell. Arrange the fruit decoratively on top.
Serves 4 to 6

◆ *Spaghetti Dolce* ◆

SPIKE MILLIGAN, COMEDIAN

1lb (500g) spaghetti
5fl oz (150ml) double cream

2 tablespoons brandy
Castor sugar to taste

Cook the spaghetti in boiling water for about 8 minutes, or until *al dente*. Meanwhile mix together the cream, brandy and castor sugar. When the spaghetti is ready, pour the cream mixture over and serve immediately.
Serves 4

◆ *Compote* ◆

JANET ELLIS OF *BLUE PETER*

1 large bunch of seedless grapes,
    peeled
1 medium pineapple, cored,
    peeled and cut into chunks
1–2 eating apples, peeled, cored
    and sliced

8oz (250g) cherries, peeled,
    halved and stoned
Liqueur (brandy, Kirsch, etc.)
Sugar

Put all the fruit into a large bowl with enough liqueur to moisten. Add sugar to taste. Place in the refrigerator and leave for 3 to 4 hours before serving. Simple and delicious.
Serves 4 to 6

◆ *Pears in Coffee* ◆

JUNE WHITFIELD, COMEDIENNE

4 large firm pears, peeled, halved
    and cored
2oz (50g) Demerara sugar

10fl oz (300ml) made-up coffee
3 tablespoons Tia Maria
Double cream to serve

Pre-heat the oven to gas mark 3, 325°F (170°C).
    Place the pears flat side down in an ovenproof dish and sprinkle with the sugar. Pour in the coffee and liqueur, cover and bake in the oven for about 35 minutes until just tender. Take care not to over-cook. Serve cold with lots of cream.
    The pears may be stored in the refrigerator for up to 1 week.
Serves 6 to 8

◆ *Creamed Rice with Apricot Purée* ◆

DELIA SMITH, COOKERY WRITER

3oz (75g) short-grain rice
1–1¼ pints (600–750ml) milk
1½ tablespoons sugar
5fl oz (150ml) double cream
2–3 drops vanilla essence

3oz (75g) dried apricots, soaked
   overnight in 10fl oz (300ml)
   water
A little lemon juice and extra
   sugar

First measure the rice into a saucepan and pour in 1 pint (600ml) of the milk. Add 1½ tablespoons sugar, bring to the boil and simmer gently for 30 minutes or until the rice is absolutely tender and the milk has been absorbed – watch it carefully during the latter stages as it can burn easily. Add a little more milk if the rice seems to need a little more cooking. Then remove from the heat and leave to cool for 10 minutes.

Whip the cream to the 'floppy' stage and fold into the cooled rice, together with the vanilla essence. Pour the mixture into a 1–1¼ pint (600–750ml) pudding basin and chill in the refrigerator until firm.

To make the apricot purée, place the soaked apricots (and their soaking water) in a small pan, bring to the boil, cover and simmer for about 10 minutes, or until the apricots are tender. Then either liquidize in a blender or rub through a sieve. Taste and flavour the purée with a little lemon juice and sugar as required – and if it is too thick, thin it down with a little water.

To serve, unmould the rice pudding on to a plate and serve with the apricot purée poured over.

Serves 2 to 3

◆ *Transkei Mud* ◆

CLIFF RICHARD, SINGER

1 × 14 oz (400g) tin condensed
   milk
10fl oz (300ml) double cream
6–7oz (175–200ml) digestive
   biscuits (crumbled)

1 bar mint chocolate (Aero or
   Bitz)

First caramelize the condensed milk. Put the unopened tin in a pan, cover well with water, bring to the boil and simmer for 1½ hours. Check occasionally that there is still plenty of water in the pan and top up as necessary. Alternatively, caramelize in a pressure cooker for 20 minutes.

Whip the cream until it stands in soft peaks. Slowly add the caramelized condensed milk, a spoonful at a time, and mix together thoroughly. Grate two-thirds of the mint chocolate into the mixture and combine well. In a glass bowl put a layer of one third of the digestive biscuits followed by a layer of one third of the cream mixture, and repeat twice more so that you have three layers of each. Stand in the refrigerator overnight. Grate the remaining mint chocolate over the dish before serving.

Serves 6

◆ *Elderflower Fritters* ◆

LONDON HILTON HOTEL

For the fritters:
12 medium-sized elderflowers
2 egg yolks
Pinch of salt
A little grated lemon rind
1oz (25g) sugar
3oz (75g) flour
2fl oz (50ml) milk
2fl oz (50ml) strong lager
3 egg whites
Clarified butter for deep-frying
4fl oz (125ml) gooseberry cream
   sauce to serve

For the gooseberry sauce:
12oz (350g) gooseberries
1oz (25g) sugar
1oz (25g) butter
Salt and pepper
¼ level teaspoon ground nutmeg
2 tablespoons lightly whipped
   double cream

Wash and dry the elderflowers. Place the egg yolks, salt, lemon rind and sugar into a mixing bowl and stir until smooth, then add the flour, milk and lager and continue stirring until completely mixed. Cover the bowl and leave to rest in a cool place before using. When you are ready to cook, beat the egg whites until stiff but not dry and fold into the batter mixture. Dip the elderflowers into the batter and deep-fry in hot clarified butter. Dress with the gooseberry cream sauce and serve immediately.

To make the gooseberry sauce, simmer the topped and tailed gooseberries in ¼ pint (150ml) water for 4 to 5 minutes, until tender and pulped. Drain and rub through a sieve or purée in a blender. Add sugar, butter, salt, pepper and nutmeg. Fold in lightly whipped double cream.
Serves 4

◆ *Pishides (Fritters)* ◆

FRANÇOISE BONDONNEAU, HEAD OF FRENCH,
FARRINGTONS SCHOOL

For the syrup:
2 cups sugar
Juice of ½ lemon
1 dessertspoon rose water

For the dough:
3 cups flour
3 tablespoons vegetable oil

For the filling:
2 cups chopped almonds
2 cups sugar
1 tablespoon cinnamon

Oil for deep-frying

To make the syrup, put the sugar in a pan with 10fl oz (300ml) water and bring gently to the boil, stirring all the time. Let it boil for 2 to 3 minutes, then remove from the heat and stir in the lemon juice and rose water. Leave to cool.

To make the dough, sift the flour into bowl, make a well in the centre and pour in the oil. Rub this into the flour. Add enough water to make a firm dough. Knead the dough well and allow to rest. Then divide it into two and roll out into two rectangles about ⅛in. (3mm) thick.

To make the filling, mix all the ingredients together. Reserve a little of the filling mixture and sprinkle the rest over one pastry rectangle. Cover with the other. Roll the pastry up like a Swiss roll to form a long sausage. Cut slices about ½in. (13mm) thick from the roll and form into flat, round shapes.

Heat the oil and deep-fry the fritters until golden brown. Lift them from the oil and immerse them in the syrup. Lift from the syrup and serve with a sprinkling of the reserved filling mixture.
Serves 4 to 6

◆ *Weinachts Creme* ◆

JAYNE TORVILL AND CHRISTOPHER DEAN, SKATERS

4oz (125g) prunes, stoned and
  finely chopped
Rum
10fl oz (300ml) milk
2 eggs
2 egg yolks
5oz (150g) castor sugar

2 drops vanilla essence
10fl oz (300ml) whipping or
  double cream

For the praline:
3oz (75g) walnuts, coarsely
  chopped
4oz (125g) granulated sugar

Soak the prunes in the rum for several hours – preferably overnight.
Drain.

To make the praline, place the walnuts in a pan with the granulated
sugar over a moderate heat. Stir occasionally. When the sugar has
caramelized and coated the walnuts, pour on to a greased baking sheet
and leave to set. Crush between two sheets of greaseproof paper, using a
rolling pin.

Place the milk, eggs, egg yolks, castor sugar and vanilla essence in a
bowl over a pan of gently simmering water and whisk with an electric
beater until thick – when the beater is raised from the mixture, peaks
should remain on the surface for 2 seconds. Remove from the heat, and
continue whisking until cold. Half-whip the cream and fold into the
whisked mixture with the prunes. Chill in the refrigerator.

Sprinkle the walnut praline over the dish to serve, or hand it
separately in a bowl.
Serves 4 to 6

◆ *Coconut Tartlets* ◆

MOLLIE SUGDEN, COMEDIENNE

4oz (125g) shortcrust pastry
Jam
2oz (50g) butter

2oz (50g) castor sugar
2oz (50g) desiccated coconut
½ egg, beaten

Pre-heat the oven to gas mark 5, 375°F (190°C).

Roll out the pastry thinly and line 12 patty tins. Place a little jam in each. Cream the butter and sugar, and stir in the beaten egg and coconut. Mix well. Divide the mixture between the pastry cases. Bake in the oven for about 15 minutes.

Makes 12

◆ *Individual Apple Tarts* ◆

KATIE STEWART, COOKERY WRITER

1 × 13oz (368g) packet frozen puff
  pastry, thawed
3 dessert apples
Beaten egg to glaze

Icing sugar
2 tablespoons apricot jam
Lemon juice

Dust a cool working surface with flour and roll out the puff pastry to a thickness of about ¼in. (6mm). You require six circles of pastry approximately 4in. (10cm) in circumference, so try to guide the pastry to an oblong approximately 8in. (20cm) wide and 12in. (30cm) long. Place the rolled pastry on a baking sheet and chill in the refrigerator for about 30 minutes.

Heat the oven to gas mark 6, 400°F (200°C).

With a 4in. (10cm) cutter, stamp out six pastry circles and transfer to a baking sheet that has been rinsed with cold water.

Peel the apples, leaving them whole, and, with an apple corer, remove the cores. Now cut each apple in half and then slice each half evenly, holding them together in the correct order.

Transfer one half apple to the centre of each pastry circle. Brush the pastry edges with beaten egg. Bake the apple tarts in the oven for 30 minutes. The pastry will rise around the apple to form a border and the apple slices will cook through.

When each tart is risen, dust generously with icing sugar and return to the oven for a further 5 minutes to glaze. Alternatively, set the tarts under a hot grill until the sugar has caramelized.

Heat the apricot jam with a squeeze of lemon juice in a saucepan until melted and bubbling. For a final touch, glaze the apple lightly with the jam. Serve hot with cream.

Serves 6

◆ *Almond Chocolate Bombe* ◆

CHRIS SMITH, HAMPSHIRE AND ENGLAND CRICKETER

1 small chocolate sponge cake
2 tablespoons Amaretto or similar
   liqueur
2oz (50g) slivered almonds,
   toasted, to serve

For the dark parfait:
1½oz (40g) castor sugar
4oz (125g) plain chocolate
2 egg yolks
7½fl oz (225ml) double cream

For the white parfait:
2oz (50g) castor sugar
6oz (175g) white chocolate,
   chopped
3 egg yolks
10fl oz (300ml) double cream

To make the dark parfait, dissolve the sugar in 3 tablespoons water and boil for 1 to 2 minutes. Put the chocolate in a food processor or blender, switch on, then pour the hot syrup through the feed tube. When well blended, add the egg yolks one at a time. Allow to cool. Whip the cream until it stands in soft peaks, and fold into the mixture. Place in the freezer until half-frozen, then spread the mixture over the base and sides of a 2 pint (1 litre) pudding basin to form an even layer. Freeze until firm.

Make the white parfait in the same way, dissolving the sugar in 4 tablespoons water.

Sprinkle the chocolate sponge cake with 2 tablespoons liqueur and cut into fingers. Line the chocolate-coated basin with a layer of sponge fingers and freeze again until firm. Spoon the white parfait mixture into the centre of the lined basin and smooth the surface. Cover and freeze again.

To serve, dip the basin briefly in hot water, then turn out on to a plate and sprinkle with slivered almonds.

Serves 4 to 6

◆ *Chocolate Peanut Sauce* ◆

SARAH LOVETT-SMITH, FARRINGTONS SCHOOL PUPIL

1 large bar chocolate
5 tablespoons crunchy peanut
    butter

5 tablespoons milk

Melt the chocolate in a bowl resting over a pan of simmering water. Add the peanut butter and milk and stir constantly until well mixed and heated through. This is delicious poured over cooked pears or ice cream.

◆ *Surprise Truffles* ◆

SARAH LOVETT-SMITH, FARRINGTONS SCHOOL PUPIL

For the praline:
2oz (50g) chopped nuts: almonds,
    hazelnuts or a mixture
2oz (50g) granulated sugar

For the truffles:
4oz (125g) plain or milk chocolate
1oz (25g) butter
Liqueur (optional)
Chocolate vermicelli or
    desiccated coconut

First make the praline. Put the nuts and sugar in a pan and heat gently until the sugar melts. When turning a pale golden colour, stir and continue to cook until well browned. Turn on to a greased baking sheet and leave until cold, then grind or crush finely.

To make the truffles, melt the chocolate and butter together over a low heat. Remove from the heat and stir in the praline and liqueur (if using). Leave until firm – not hard– then roll into small balls with the hands and toss in the vermicelli or coconut.
Makes about 16

◆Cakes
& Bread◆

◆ *Welsh Cakes* ◆

RT HON NEIL KINNOCK, MP, LEADER OF THE LABOUR PARTY

8oz (250g) self-raising flour
4oz (125g) butter or margarine
3oz (75g) currants

3oz (75g) castor sugar
1 large egg, beaten
Milk

Sift the flour into a bowl and rub in the butter or margarine with the fingertips. When the mixture resembles breadcrumbs, add the currants and sugar. Mix in the egg. Use your hands to form the mixture into a dough and add a little milk if it is too dry. Transfer the dough to a floured working surface or board. Roll it out to about ¼in. (6mm) thick and cut it into rounds with a 2in. (5cm) cutter.

Traditionally a heavy griddle is used to cook Welsh cakes but a good solid frying pan will do. Heat the griddle or frying pan over a medium heat and cook the cakes for about 2 to 3 minutes on each side. Make sure that they are cooked through and are a golden brown colour.

Serve them as they are or buttered with Welsh butter or spread with honey.

◆ *Strones (Oatcakes)* ◆

JAMES GALWAY, FLAUTIST

For hundreds of year in Ulster, a large strone was made in the shape of a cross to celebrate the feast of St Brigit. Strones were traditionally served hot and dripping with freshly made butter.

8oz (250g) oatmeal	Pinch of salt
Pinch of baking powder	1 teaspoon bacon fat

Pre-heat the oven to gas mark 4, 350°F (180°C).

Sift the oatmeal, baking powder and salt into a bowl. Melt the fat in a little boiling water, add to the bowl and use to mix the dry ingredients to a stiff dough. Scatter more oatmeal over it and knead thoroughly. Roll out as thinly as possible into a circle. Put on a greased baking sheet. Cut a cross on the top so that, when cooked, the oatcake can easily be broken into quarters, the traditional farls. Bake in the oven for about 20 minutes. Serve with lots of butter.
Makes 4

◆ *Malt Loaf* ◆

HANNAH GORDON, ACTRESS

This is a good recipe for children to make because it's simple. I usually use 81 per cent wholemeal self-raising flour.

2 cups self-raising flour	1 cup dark soft brown sugar
Pinch of salt	1 tablespoon black treacle,
1 cup dried fruit (currants and/or raisins)	dissolved in 1 cup warm milk

Pre-heat the oven to gas mark 4, 350°F (180°C).

Sift the flour and salt into a bowl. Add all the other ingredients and mix well with a metal spoon. Put the mixture into a 1lb (500g) greased loaf tin. Bake in the oven for 1 hour. Leave in the tin for a few minutes after removing from the oven, then tip out and cool on a wire rack. Serve sliced and buttered.

Makes a 1lb loaf

◆ *Selkirk Bannocks* ◆

RT HON DAVID STEEL, MP, LEADER OF THE LIBERAL PARTY

2oz (50g) polyunsaturated
  margarine
5fl oz (150ml) skimmed milk
2 teaspoons dried yeast

2oz (50g) brown sugar
8oz (250g) strong flour
4oz (125g) sultanas

Heat the margarine and milk until tepid in a small pan, then pour on to the yeast in a small bowl. Stir in 1 teaspoon of the sugar and leave in a warm place for about 10 minutes, until frothy.

Sift the flour into a warmed bowl and stir in the remaining sugar and sultanas. Add the yeast liquid and knead the dough for 5 minutes. Leave to rise, covered with a damp cloth or small sheet of polythene, in a warm place for about 1 hour until doubled in size. Knead the dough again and divide it into two. Shape each piece into a circle and put on an oiled baking tray. Leave to rise again in a warm place for about 20 minutes.

Meanwhile, heat the oven to gas mark 7, 425°F (220°C). Bake the bannocks in the oven for 15 minutes, then reduce the heat to gas mark 5, 375°F (190°C) for a further 15 to 20 minutes. Check that the bannocks are ready by tapping the base, which should sound hollow. Cool the bannocks on a wire tray.

Makes 2 large bannocks, enough to serve 8

◆ *Spicy Buttermilk Coffee Cake* ◆

STEVE OVETT, ATHLETE

2¼ cups flour
½ teaspoon salt
2 teaspoons cinnamon
¼ teaspoon ground ginger
1 cup brown sugar
¾ cup white sugar

¾ cup corn oil
1 cup chopped nuts
1 teaspoon baking soda
1 teaspoon baking powder
1 egg, beaten
1 cup buttermilk

Pre-heat the oven to gas mark 4, 350°F (180°C).

Sift the flour, salt, 1 teaspoon of the cinnamon and the ginger into a large bowl and add both sugars and the corn oil. Remove ¾ cup of this mixture and to it add the nuts and the remaining cinnamon. Mix well and set aside.

To the remaining batter, add the baking soda, baking powder, egg and buttermilk. Mix just to combine the ingredients – no more. (Small lumps in the batter are OK.) Pour into a well greased 9in. × 12in. (23cm × 30cm) baking tin. Sprinkle the nut mixture evenly over the top. Bake in the oven for 40 to 45 minutes.

Serves 6 to 8

◆ *Toffee Shortbread* ◆

WENDY RICHARD OF EASTENDERS

For the shortbread:
8oz (250g) self-raising flour.
2oz (50g) soft brown sugar
5oz (150g) margarine

4oz (125g) plain chocolate

For the toffee:
4oz (125g) margarine
2 tablespoons golden syrup
3oz (75g) soft brown sugar
1 × 7oz (200g) tin condensed milk

Pre-heat the oven to gas mark 3, 325°F (170°C).

To make the shortbread, sift the flour into a bowl and rub in the margarine with the fingertips until the mixture resembles breadcrumbs – do not mix until solid. Stir in the sugar thoroughly. Press the mixture into a 9in. × 7in. (23cm × 18cm) tin and bake in the oven for 25 minutes.

To make the toffee, put all the ingredients in a pan over medium heat and cook until the mixture forms a small ball when a little is dropped into a cup of cold water. Pour over the shortbread.

Melt the chocolate in a basin resting over a pan of simmering water. Spread the chocolate over the toffee layer and leave to set. Cut into squares to serve.

Serves 8

◆ *Yorkshire Apple Cake* ◆

DIANA BRITTAN, WIFE OF RT HON LEON BRITTAN, MP

2lb (1kg) cooking apples
A little sugar
1 slice of lemon
2 cloves
8oz (250g) margarine
8oz (250g) castor sugar
2 eggs

4oz (125g) plain flour
3oz (75g) blanched almonds
Few drops of almond essence
  (optional)
Few thin slices of marzipan
  (optional)

Make a compote with the cooking apples, sugar (it should not be very sweet), lemon slice and cloves. Half-cook and allow to cool.

Heat the oven to gas mark 3, 325°F (170°C).

Beat the margarine and sugar till well creamed. Beat in the eggs one at a time. Fold in the flour and almonds, keeping a few back for decoration. Add the almond essence (if using). Put half the mixture at the bottom of a loose-bottomed cake tin, spread the apple compote over, lay on a few very thin slices of marzipan (if desired), then put the rest of the cake mixture on top of that. Decorate with the remaining almonds. Bake in the oven for 1¼ hours, placing a baking sheet on the shelf below to catch any drips.

This may be eaten cold, but is best lukewarm, served with whipped cream.

Serves about 8

◆ *Dorset Apple Cake* ◆

JANET WAYMARK, HEAD OF GEOGRAPHY, FARRINGTONS SCHOOL

This is one of a variety of recipes for Dorset Apple Cake, and is given as a reminder of geography field trips which Farringtonians have enjoyed at Lyme Regis. The cake does not keep very well – but then it doesn't have to!

3oz (75g) butter
6oz (175g) castor sugar
Grated orange rind to taste
2 eggs, beaten
8oz (250g) self-raising flour

½ teaspoon cinnamon (optional)
1oz (25g) chopped mixed peel
1lb (500g) stewed apples, drained
2 tablespoons milk (optional)
Granulated sugar

Pre-heat the oven to gas mark 4, 350°F (180°C).

Cream the butter, castor sugar and orange rind until light and fluffy. Beat in the eggs, adding 1 tablespoon of the flour (to which has been added the cinnamon if liked). Fold in the rest of the flour followed by the peel, apples and milk (if needed) to form a mixture a little stiffer than a dropping consistency. Turn into an 8in. (20cm) greased cake tin, shake granulated sugar over the top, and bake in the oven for about 50 minutes, until firm to the touch and golden brown.

The cake may be eaten hot with cream or ice cream as a pudding, or cold for tea.

Serves 8

◆ German Apple Cake ◆

SIMON GROOM OF *BLUE PETER*

4oz (125g) butter
4oz (125g) sugar
2–3 eggs (depending on size)
4 drops of lemon flavouring
7oz (200g) self-raising flour

1–4 tablespoons milk
1lb (500g) apples, peeled, cored
   and quartered
Icing sugar

Pre-heat the oven to gas mark 4, 350°F (180°C).
   Beat the butter and sugar together until light and creamy. Beat in the eggs, one at a time. Add the lemon flavouring. Fold in the flour and add the milk a little at a time, until the mixture is of a soft, dropping consistency. Put the mixture into a greased 8in. (20cm) cake tin. Score the apples with a knife to decorate, and place them on the top of the mixture with the scored surface uppermost. Bake in the oven for about 45 minutes or until golden brown. Dust with icing sugar before serving.
Serves 8

◆ Krispie Cake ◆

ANDREW GARDNER, TELEVISION JOURNALIST

4oz (125g) margarine
4oz (125g) marshmallows

4oz (125g) toffee
6oz (175g) Rice Krispies

Put the margarine, marshmallows and toffee into a large saucepan and rest this on top of an even larger saucepan of simmering water. Stir until melted. Add the Rice Krispies 2oz (50g) at a time and mix well.
   Turn out into an oblong dish. Press down well while still soft and mark into squares. Put into the refrigerator for 2 hours until set. Store in an airtight tin.
Serves 8

❖ *Uncooked Chocolate Cake* ❖

PATRICIA SHERIDAN,
HEAD OF FARRINGTONS JUNIOR SCHOOL

3–4oz (75–125g) butter or
   margarine
3oz (75g) sugar
1 cup mixed dried fruit
1 heaped teaspoon cocoa (or more
   to taste)

6oz (175g) digestive or other plain
   biscuits, crushed
1 egg, beaten
Chocolate, melted

Melt the butter and sugar in a pan over a low heat. Stir in the fruit and cocoa and simmer for 1 minute. Remove from the heat and cool slightly. Add the crushed biscuits and beaten egg and mix well. Press into a greased flan dish and leave to set. When cold, ice with melted chocolate.
Serves 8

◆Jams
❦ Preserves ◆

◆ *Berry Jam* ◆

JULIET PLANT, FARRINGTONS SCHOOL PARENT AND
GOVERNOR'S WIFE

2lb (1kg) blackberries
2lb (1kg) elderberries

3lb (1.5kg) granulated or
preserving sugar

Strip the elderberries from their stalks and place these with the blackberries in a preserving pan. Crush the fruit with a wooden spoon to make the juice run. Bring slowly to the boil and simmer for 20 minutes. Warm the sugar and add it to the pan, stir until dissolved, then boil the jam hard for 20 minutes. When the jam has reached setting point (see page 132), pour into sterilized jam jars. Cover and label, and store in a cool place.

Makes about 6lb (2.75kg)

◆ *Lime Marmalade* ◆

JANET WAYMARK, HEAD OF GEOGRAPHY, FARRINGTONS
SCHOOL

2lb (1kg) limes

4lb (2kg) sugar

Simmer the whole limes in 4 pints (2.3 litres) water in a lidded pan until soft – about 2 hours. Remove the limes and shred by hand, discarding the pips. Return the fruit to the pan and, if the contents have not been reduced by a third, continue to simmer until they have. Add the sugar, simmer until dissolved, then test for a set (see page 132). Put into sterilized jars, cover and label. Store in a cool place.

Makes about 8lb (3.7kg)

◆ *Plum and Almond Preserve* ◆

SUE LAWLEY, TELEVISION JOURNALIST

3lb (1.5kg) plums, halved and
  stoned

3lb (1.5kg) preserving sugar
2oz (50g) almonds, skinned

Put the plums in a large pan with 1 pint (600ml) cold water and simmer for 1 hour or until they are soft. Stir in the sugar and continue to heat gently until the sugar has dissolved. Bring the mixture to the boil and boil hard for about 15 minutes or until the jam has reached setting point. Take the pan off the heat while you test. (Test for a set by putting a little jam on a cold saucer and letting it cool in the fridge. Push your finger through it, and if the jam wrinkles, it is ready.)

Stir in the almonds and allow the jam to cool for 15 minutes. Stir again to prevent the almonds rising before putting it into heated sterilized jars. Cover and label, and store in a cool place.
Makes 5lb (2.25kg)

Cook's tip: To skin almonds, place them in a pan of cold water and bring to the boil. Drain as soon as the water boils and cover with cold water. As soon as the almonds are cool enough to handle, slip off the skins between your thumb and forefinger.

◆ *Grandma Casely's Seville Orange Marmalade* ◆

EIRA CUMING, HEAD OF HOME ECONOMICS, FARRINGTONS
SCHOOL

2lb (1kg) Seville oranges   4lb (2kg) sugar

Wash the oranges thoroughly and peel them. Slice the peel very thinly.
Cut the peeled fruit in half and slice, removing the pips. Put the pips
into a muslin bag and secure well.

Weigh the preserving pan. Put the orange peel, pip bag, sliced
oranges and 6 pints (3.4 litres) water into the pan, bring to the boil and
simmer for 1½ to 2½ hours, until the peel is tender or until the contents
of the pan weigh 4lb (2kg). This is important if you want a good flavour to
the marmalade.

Off the heat, remove the pip bag. Add the sugar and stir until
dissolved. Return to the heat and boil rapidly for 10 to 15 minutes. Test
for a set (see page 132). When the marmalade is at setting point, remove
from the heat and allow to stand for 5 minutes before putting into
sterilized jars. Cover, label and store in a cool place.

Do not think you can improve the flavour by adding a proportion of
lemons or sweet oranges. This marmalade should be made solely from
Seville sour oranges.

Makes about 8lb (3.7kg)

◆ *Sweet Orange Ginger Marmalade* ◆

JANET WAYMARK, HEAD OF GEOGRAPHY, FARRINGTONS SCHOOL

2lb (1kg) sweet oranges
1 large lemon
12oz (350g) crystallized ginger,
   chopped

½ teaspoon ground ginger
4lb (2kg) sugar

Shred the peel and flesh of the oranges, including the pith but removing any tough sections round the central stem. Reserve the pips. (The best results are achieved with an attachment to a table-top mincer, but otherwise hand-cut or mince in the usual way.) Squeeze the juice from the lemon and reserve the pips. Put the orange and lemon pips into a muslin bag and secure well.

Pour 4 pints (2.3 litres) water into a preserving pan and add the lemon juice and the shredded oranges. Suspend the pip bag in the pan. Bring to the boil and simmer until the contents of the pan have been reduced by about one third. Remove the pip bag. Add the crystallized ginger, ground ginger and sugar, and continue to simmer until the marmalade has reached setting point (see page 132). Put into sterilized jars, cover and label. Store in a cool place.

Makes about 8lb (3.7kg)

◆ *Sweet Mango Chutney* ◆

SHEILA BROWN, GEOGRAPHY TEACHER, FARRINGTONS
SCHOOL

8–10 large unripe mangoes
3 teaspoons salt
8 large dried chillies
1½ pints (850ml) malt vinegar
5 cloves of garlic

2oz (50g) root ginger, peeled and
   chopped
1 teaspoon garam masala
1lb (500g) sugar
1 cup sultanas or seedless raisins

Peel the mangoes and slice thickly, discarding the seeds. Put the mango slices in a large bowl and sprinkle with salt.

Remove the stalks and seeds from the chillies, soak them in a little of the vinegar for 10 minutes, then put into the goblet of an electric blender with the garlic and ginger and blend. It does not matter if small pieces of chilli remain unbroken.

If a blender is not available, pound the soaked chillies with a pestle and mortar and grate the cloves of garlic and the peeled ginger on a fine grater.

Put the remaining vinegar into an enamel or stainless steel pan with the blended mixture, garam masala and sugar, and bring to the boil. Simmer, uncovered, for 15 minutes. Add the mangoes and sultanas or raisins, and simmer until thick and syrupy. Cool and put into sterilized bottles. Seal airtight and label. Store in a cool place.
Makes about 5lb (2.25kg)

Note: 3lb (1.5kg) green apples, apricots or other suitable fruit may be used in place of mangoes.

◆ *Apple Chutney* ◆

PENELOPE KEITH, ACTRESS

4lb (2kg) windfall apples, peeled,
   cored and roughly chopped
1lb (500g) sultanas
1 pint (600ml) vinegar
1 teaspoon ground ginger

1 clove of garlic, chopped
1lb (500g) onions, chopped
1lb (500g) soft brown sugar
1 teaspoon salt
½ teaspoon black pepper

Put all the ingredients in a large pan, bring to the boil and simmer gently for 3 to 4 hours until the chutney is thick and brown. Put into sterilized jars while still hot. Cover, label and store in a cool place.
Makes about 7lb (3.25kg)

◆*The Lighter Touch!*◆

◆ *Cockle Sandwich* ◆

JULIE WALTERS, ACTRESS AND COMEDIENNE

Fresh cockles
2 slices brown bread

Butter or margarine
Black pepper

Butter the bread, spread 1 slice with cockles, sprinkle with pepper and lay the other slice of bread on top!

◆ *Cornflakes (Breakfast Dish)* ◆

JOHN CLEESE, ACTOR AND COMEDIAN

1 Buy a packet of cornflakes;
2 Open the cardboard box;
3 Open the sort of plastic packet inside the box;
4 Pour the contents (sort of yellowy brownish bits of things) on to a plate;
5 Buy a bottle of milk;
6 Take the top off the thin end of the bottle;
7 Invert the bottle gently over the cornflakes, making sure that the milk does not go over the edge of the plate.

It's very simple to make and absolutely delicious. An alternative is to use Coca-cola instead of milk. Add basil as required.

◆ *Stuffed Camel* ◆

ROY CASTLE,
COMEDIAN, SINGER, DANCER, MUSICIAN, ETC.

72 hard-boiled eggs, shelled, stuffed into....................................
24 fish, headed and tailed, stuffed into ....
6 chickens, de-feathered, etc., stuffed into................................
1 sheep, de-fleeced, etc., stuffed into ....
1 camel

Cook in the oven at gas mark 5, 375°F (190°C) for nine days or until tender. Eaten only at Bedouin wedding feasts.
It's a record bank-balance breaker.
PS. Don't forget to say Grace!!

◆ *Beans on Toast* ◆

DESMOND LYNAM, PRESENTER OF *GRANDSTAND*

1 Take 1 small tin of Heinz baked beans.
2 Carefully open said tin, making sure to avoid cutting finger.
3 Empty contents into a saucepan.
4 Heat gradually, taking care not to overcook.
5 Serve on already prepared toast.
6 Spice to taste.

Delicious, nutritious and lots of roughage.

◆ *Millionaire's Munch* ◆

JIMMY SAVILE,
DISC JOCKEY AND TELEVISION PERSONALITY

1 tin of tomato soup   1 tin of anything of your choice
1 tin of beans

Place these in a pan. Heat. Eat straight from the pan. Do not burn yourself on the hot pan.
    Live like this and you too can be rich in a year!

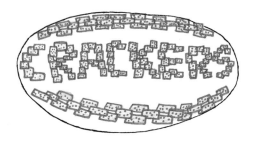

◆ *Acknowledgements* ◆

The publishers are most grateful to the following pupils of Farringtons School for supplying illustrations which appear in this book: Rebecca Wright, front of jacket and page 132; Alice Wong, jacket flap and pages 7, 9, 61; Danielle Burrell, title page; Lucy Symmons, page 4; Chika Shigeyasu, pages 11, 125; Pinky Patel, page 15; Sam Barling, page 22; Mary Osei-Gyau, page 27; Barbara Southey, pages 30, 84; Katherine Webster, pages 34, 39, 45, 51, 52, 53, 63, 67, 73, 78, 80, 91, 100; Nicola Yates-Bell, pages 37, 47, 65, 79, 82, 83, 86, 87, 117, 122; Antonia Hughes, pages 55, 136; Judy Koloko, page 59; Lisa Edgar, page 77; Susan Hinds, page 89; Tracey Shaw, page 101; Stephanie Lewis, pages 104, 127; Katy Summerfield, page 105; Alexandra Collins, page 109; Sarah Patton, page 113; Olwen Jones, page 119; Sandeep Panesar, page 123; Clare Tompsett, page 129; Karen Bennett and Katie Gorman, page's 137, 144; Roshika Singh, page 141; Mayo Kanno, page 143.

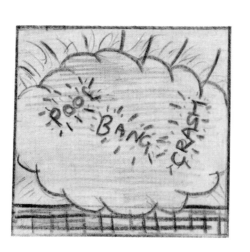